A NEW SUNRISE

One Man's Inspirational Journey from Surviving the Unimaginable Trauma of Terrorism to a Life of Meaning and Purpose

by

Jacob Kimchy

KIMCHY
PRESS

Cover Design: Janis Dworkis
Cover Photograph: Adi Lior

Library of Congress Control Number: 2015904854.

ISBN 978-0-9961953-0-0

For my mother
Sarah Kimchy,
my superhero who inspires me every day
and shows me the importance of life.

For my late father
Rami Kimchy,
who motivates me and
pushes me to become a better person
to continue what he left here in the world.

For survivors of trauma everywhere.

For all the victims who are no longer with us.

CONTENTS

1	Coming Full Circle	1
2	The Dream	5
3	The Accident	7
4	My Father's Resilience	30
5	Untouchable	45
6	Life on a Roll	63
7	The Unimaginable	71
8	Lost	87
9	A Ray of Light	113
10	A New Family	142
11	Finding One Heart	155
12	Lifting Up Teens of Terrorism	180
13	My New Sunrise	195
	Dear Friends	217
	Acknowledgments	219
	About the Author	220

The names of all minor children and some adults have been changed to protect privacy.

CHAPTER ONE
Coming Full Circle

"Jacob, good morning!" Nina waved when she saw me at our usual table, a blast of frigid air entering the tiny shop with her. "Do you want anything?"

"No, no. Go ahead and get in line," I said, showing her my coffee and cake.

Nina looked wonderful, as always. She was a beautiful woman in her 40s — at least 12 years older than me — smartly dressed, briefcase always on her shoulder. I had thoroughly enjoyed the many times we had met just like this, in a coffee shop or restaurant, just two people enjoying a normal conversation. But this would be the last time we would see each other before she moved. Nina had been hoping to get out of New York for a long time. She finally had found a wonderful job in a warmer climate, and I was thrilled for her.

When she made her way over to the table, we greeted each other with a hug.

"I can't believe this is our last time talking together," she said.

"Well, it's not like we can never call on the phone again, you know."

"I know. But it's not the same."

She was right. "No, it's not the same. But if you ever need to talk, Nina, you know I'm always here for you."

"I know you are." She smiled. We went on for a bit about the suddenly cold weather and about the Yankees losing to Detroit in the playoffs. Then she said, "Jacob, you heard the news, right?"

I looked at Nina and nodded my head. "Yes, I heard." A small plane had crashed into an apartment building in Manhattan the previous day. The two people in the plane had been killed, and more than 20 people had been injured.

"Did you see pictures of the building?" she asked.

"I did."

"And did you hear how many firefighters were injured?"

"Yes, I did. Quite a few." I took a sip of my coffee and then asked, "Nina, how are you feeling today?"

"I don't know," she said shaking her head and staring down at the table. She took a deep breath. "Well, that's not exactly true. I feel terrified."

"I can understand that. It makes sense, don't you think? I think such a terrible accident and the pictures of it scared an awful lot of people."

She nodded. "I know. But I never wanted to see that again. Ever."

"I know you didn't."

Nina had been in Brooklyn on the clear, beautiful morning of September 11, 2001, staring out her window at the World Trade Center. She had seen the first plane crash into the North Tower and the second plane crash into the South Tower. She had watched when both buildings collapsed. She has witnessed the deaths of thousands.

Everything in her life seemed to stop for Nina after that. She kept seeing the buildings, the fire, the smoke over and over. She found she couldn't sleep and could barely eat. She kept the drapes permanently closed to make sure she wouldn't accidentally look outside. She would sweat just riding in her building's elevator. She finally moved out.

Initially, her parents, siblings, and friends were all interested in hearing her tell and retell the story of that day. But after a few weeks, they were finished, ready to move on.

"What's wrong with you?" her parents would ask when Nina would burst into tears. "It's not like you lost anyone you knew that day. And you didn't get injured."

"But I watched thousands of people die. You don't understand. Thousands, in a matter of minutes."

"The whole world watched it, Nina. We all saw it on the news. It affected all of us. But it's time to get over it. It's been long enough."

Nina was my neighbor when I first moved to New York from Israel. When she told me what she had witnessed, I encouraged her to come to the Survivors' Circles I was establishing. In the Circles, she was finally able to put into words what she had kept so tightly inside for years.

"I felt like I would never get over what I saw," she said. "I didn't think I could ever look at a tall building again or even see such a blue sky as we had that day without my heart pounding and pounding. I was so scared all the time. Every minute. I constantly felt that I was having a heart attack. I could hardly breathe. I thought I would die."

"You are a victim of terrorism, Nina," our group facilitator said slowly. "There is no human being on this earth who could witness the death of so many and not be traumatized."

Nina talked about what she had seen and felt, all of it. She cried, and then she talked some more. Little by little, she opened up to let out some of the poison that had been haunting her for years. She continued to attend the Survivors' Circles, but I also offered to meet with her one-on-one.

At first, we spoke about nothing but 9/11 and her feelings, her fears.

"Not all victims wear a scar on their forehead for all of us to see," I told her. "Sometimes the scar is written on every corner of a person's soul and in their deepest, most permanent memories — whether they were physically hurt themselves or witnessed such a crime from miles away."

But over time, we also talked about anything else that would come up in any normal conversation between friends — sports, what we liked about New York, our families, our work.

And now, here we were, our last time together before Nina's move. We talked about the airplane accident a bit longer, her new job, her new apartment. And then it was time to leave.

"You can call me any time at all," I told her.

"I know." And we gave each other a big hug. "Jacob, I'll be fine. I know I will be. But I also know that it will never be completely behind me. Not completely."

I smiled at her and nodded. I knew that was true. I knew.

CHAPTER TWO

The Dream

On Tuesday, May 1, 2002, I had a dream that will never leave me.

At the time, I was a 24-year-old college student studying finance and living with my parents in Rishon Lezion, Israel, where I grew up. My father drove a taxi, my mother was a homemaker, and their lives were filled with the joy of nearby grandchildren. It was a good time for my parents — for all of us, really. Life had not always been easy. But this was a good time.

That night, I dreamed I was standing at the doorway of a small, square room. During the entire dream, I never entered the room, but I was able to look in from the outside. I saw only males inside — my brother, my cousins and uncles, and a few rabbis. I could also clearly see a body wrapped in a white blanket lying on a bed in the center of the room.

All of a sudden, I realized my father was the one lying on the bed. I was looking at my father's funeral.

I was in shock. How did this happen? When did my father die? He and I had such a special bond, and our love for each other was so deep that I felt my heart breaking.

I walked closer to the doorway to get a better view. I

looked from person to person as if to ask what had happened. But I never spoke, and no one gave me any information.

Then my father's youngest brother, my Uncle Nissim, entered the room from my left. He walked toward the left side of the bed and toward the head of the body, where my other uncles were standing. When I looked at Uncle Nissim's face, he began to cry. He cried harder and harder and then leaned down to give the body a hug.

My dream ended.

As I woke up, I felt ashamed. Why was I dreaming about this? I wanted to talk to my father about it, but I felt embarrassed. And scared. Then I remembered that many Jewish people believe when you dream about the death of a person who is still alive, that person will live a long, long life. I decided to take comfort in that.

Even so, I felt such a strong desire that morning to tell my father how much I loved him. I must have told him thousands of times over the years how much he meant to me, how much I loved him, and that I would do anything in the world for him. Still, it was not enough. So that morning, I took out a pen and piece of paper and I wrote him a letter. I told him yet again how much I loved him. I described the dream and apologized for having dreamed such a thing. And I told him that no matter how good our relationship was, I wanted to grow even closer to him in the years ahead.

Feeling a bit better, I put the letter in my wallet. I was sure I would find the right time to give it to him.

CHAPTER THREE
The Accident

Where was my father?

He was 15 minutes late. And my father was *never* late.

Three times a week, I would walk home from fifth grade — school ended most days around noon — do my homework, rest, eat, and wait downstairs in front of our building for my father to pick me up at 5 o'clock for swim lessons. Rami Kimchy was never late. Everyone knew that about him.

I was a fearful and sensitive child by nature — afraid of the dark, afraid of thunder, afraid of the ocean or even a swimming pool until the summer before fifth grade, when I started swim lessons — so my first thought was that something terrible had happened to him. I imagined he had been in an accident or had gotten sick or my mother had gotten sick. Where were they? How could I help them? I felt panic starting to rise. My hands started to sweat.

Where was my father?

A girl from my school class walked by while I was standing in front of our building.

"I'm scared," I told her. "My *abba* was supposed to pick

me up for swim class. But he's not here. I think something terrible happened to him."

"You think something terrible happened just because he's late?" she asked.

"But he's *never* late."

"Really? My parents are late all the time. Don't be silly. I'm sure he's fine," she said. "But what about your coach? Will he be mad if you're late?"

I really liked my coach, and I didn't want to disappoint him. But he didn't worry me.

Where was my father?

My friend went home, and I checked my watch again. I forced myself to stand there and wait five more minutes. Then I told myself I would wait until 20 cars went by. Once I counted to 20, I decided to wait five more minutes. By that time, it was too late to make the swim class even if my father showed up right then and we drove to the pool as fast as we could. I stayed outside a little while longer — just in case — and then gave up and went home. My sister, Pazit, 15, was the only one there.

"*Abba* never picked me up for swim class," I told her. "What if something happened to him?"

Why wasn't my mother home?

"Where's *Ima?*" I asked.

But Pazit said she didn't know.

"She was with me at school at my parent/teacher conference. *Abba* was supposed to pick us up before your swim lessons, but he never came. Then all of a sudden, Uncle Joseph came running into the school and screaming for I*ma*. She ran out with him, and I came home. I don't know what's wrong."

"Uncle Joseph? Why was he there?"

If Pazit did know anything, she decided not to share it with me at that point. When my 13-year-old brother, Moshe, came home, he had no idea where our parents were.

Pazit made us something to eat, and we watched TV. We had never been left home alone without any message from our parents. Hours later, I struggled to stay awake, my heart pounding in fear as I strained to hear my parents at the door. I must have fallen asleep eventually, because I remember waking up in my bed at about 2 o'clock in the morning and hearing voices in the house — my mother and several aunts and uncles.

When I walked into the living room, everyone stopped talking. They all wiped their eyes and just looked at me.

"Where's *Abba*?" I asked them.

"Jacob, what are you doing up?" one of my aunts asked me.

"I need water. Where's my *abba*?"

"Come on, let's go in the kitchen and get you a drink. Then back to bed."

I don't know how I managed to fall asleep again.

The next morning, my mother had already left the house by the time I woke up. I came into a quiet, empty kitchen, and Moshe, Pazit and I got ourselves ready for school. My father had volunteered to chaperone a fifth-grade field trip that day, so I went to school filled with hope that he would show up as if nothing were wrong. But I never saw him.

When it was time to get on the bus, I found a place to sit by myself. I didn't want to talk to my friends. My stomach felt sick.

"Jacob, are you all right?" One of the teachers asked as she came over and put her arm around me.

No, I was not all right. Where was my father?

"I'm fine," I told her.

When I came home that afternoon, the only person in the house was one of my father's best friends, a man I knew very well. He said he needed to talk to me, so we sat on the couch in the little alcove in the living room. He started the conversation by wiping his eyes. Then he, too, put his arm around me.

"Jacob, something has happened to your father. He's in the hospital," he said.

"What happened?"

"We hope he will survive." That was the only answer he gave me.

Until that moment, I could pretend that everything would be normal again — even if my fears told me otherwise. I could pretend that I would turn a corner, and my father would be standing there with his beautiful smile, calling me to jump into his strong arms. I thought about how I would give him so many hugs and kisses while he explained his good reason for not picking me up for swim lessons.

But now, with my father's friend in tears, I knew I had been right all along. Something terrible had happened. I felt as if the ground were being washed away from underneath me.

"Your father is an angel, Jacob. He is a very, very special man," his friend said. "You know that, don't you?"

"Yes."

"And you know that all your life, your father has taken care of you, hasn't he?"

"Yes."

"But now your father is an angel who will need your help. You have an angel to take care of now, Jacob. Do you understand what I'm telling you?"

"Yes."

What I understood that day — two weeks before I would finally learn what had happened to my father — was the truth I had known every minute of my life since my first memory: My father was my world, my life. My love for him was a big, deep, aching love, and I would do anything to help him any minute of any day. Of course I would take care of him. Of course I would.

I know now that many children love their parents with the same intensity I felt that afternoon. But I also know that no one has ever been blessed with a more wonderful father than me, my sister and my brother. A kinder, gentler, more loving soul than Rami Kimchy has never been seen.

. . .

My father was only 4 years old in 1944 when his whole family left their native Bulgaria on a ship headed for Palestine, barely escaping the fate of the Jews who stayed behind. My grandparents ended up in a city called Yehud — from the word *Yehudim*, which means Jews — not far from Rishon Lezion.

As immigrants always have, they struggled to establish their new life, and nothing was easy. But my father learned the language of his new country, went to school, and grew into a handsome teenager — a blond-haired, blue-eyed young man with a strong and tanned body.

In fact, he was so handsome that when an American film crew came to Israel and saw him, the crew not only hired him as an extra but also offered him a small speaking part. My father was thrilled; a speaking part earned him a bit more money for the family.

In another time and place, maybe he would have longed for a career in the movies. But times were hard in Israel in those days, and no one could afford such dreams. Instead, he and his brother sold bourekas – delicious stuffed pastries my grandmother baked. — on the street, Later on, the brothers learned to fix sofas and they opened a small business to make a little more money.

After my father's mandatory military service — everyone in Israel serves in the military following high school:, men for three years and women for two — he went to work in the Israeli aircraft industry.

One day when he was about 25 years old, he picked up a hitchhiker named Sarah Ostroviak, a young native Israeli soldier. He had been on a mission in the south, and both were headed back to the center of the country, she to her home in Tel Aviv. They spoke for a while, and then she fell asleep while he drove. When they arrived at their destination, she thanked him and started to get out of the car.

"Wait a minute. Aren't you forgetting something?" my father asked.

"I don't think so. What?"

"Your sunglasses."

"Oh, you're right. Thanks. I would have left them in the car," she said. But when she looked for them, she couldn't find them.

"Would you like to take them with you?" my father asked with a smile.

"Of course."

"Well, you're in luck! I have your sunglasses and I'll be more than happy to give them to you — in exchange for your phone number."

And so my parents began dating.

Similar to my father's family, my mother's parents had barely escaped the Holocaust. Living in Poland during the war, my grandparents fled from the Nazis to Siberia with their daughter, my Aunt Leah, and my grandfather's son from his first marriage. My grandfather's first wife died from an illness, and his son was destined to die in their Siberian hideout at age 6. My Aunt Leah, a tiny child at the time, remembers her half-brother's funeral to this day; they buried him deep in the ground so wolves would never be able to find his body.

When the war ended, my grandparents and Aunt Leah came out of hiding and moved to Krakow, Poland. Like many thousands of Jews who survived the Holocaust, they had no money, no possessions, and no one to care for them. When they heard of organizations who were taking Jewish children to Palestine until their parents could come take care of them, my grandparents asked them to take Leah, as painful as that was to let her go.

They constantly worried about her, on a ship without them. But when they learned before too long that the children were still in Europe and had never been transported to Palestine, my grandfather knew he had to find his daughter. My grandmother waited for him in one of the Displaced Persons camps, located in Germany and safely controlled by American forces, and my grandfather eventually found Leah in a camp for Jewish children in Marseille, France.

The camp told my grandfather that if he wanted to take Leah, they immediately needed to board the *Exodus* and take the ship to Palestine. So in July 1947, while my grandmother waited in Germany — not knowing her daughter had been found — my grandfather and Leah left aboard the *Exodus*.

The *Exodus* was not allowed to dock in Palestine, and my grandfather and Leah were taken back to a camp in Marseille. My grandfather bribed an ambulance driver to hide them in the back of his ambulance and take them to the train station. From there, they took a train to Germany, found my grandmother, and emigrated together to the new State of Israel, where my mother was born.

These stories of courage, sacrifice and faith in the future — from both my father's and mother's families — were passed on to children and grandchildren, and will continue to be passed on to future generations. My grandparents sacrificed everything they had to save their families, to protect their children, in ways most of us today cannot even imagine. This courage and commitment to family is the foundation of our lineage, and we all know it.

When my parents met in 1965, my mother's unit was stationed near the southern Jordanian border. When attacks would come from Jordan, the men would stay and defend the border, and the women were supposed to run to the bunkers. But not my mother. Against orders, she would either fight alongside the men or wait out the attack in her room. But during one particular attack, my mother did run to the bunker with the other female soldiers when the attack came. To this day, she has no idea why she did that. But had she not, she certainly would have been killed. A missile landed on their barracks and exploded right in my mother's room.

My father visited her, and they walked together to the place where my mother's room had been.

"From now on," he told her, "you will always go into the bunker. Sarah. Promise me." She promised. My father picked up a few metal scraps of debris from her room. He kept those metal pieces for years.

My parents were married the next year, settled in Yehud, and my sister was born the following year. After the birth of Moshe two years later, my parents moved to Rishon Lezion. At that point, my mother retired from the military and began working at a large mall near our home.

For my brother and sister and me, it was as wonderful a childhood as anyone could ever hope for. The three of us lived together in one room, and money was tight, but our house was always filled with love and friends and family. My father's large family lived so close that we grew up with 10 first cousins on our block alone! There was always someone to play with, to compete with, to wrestle with, and always an aunt or uncle nearby if our own parents weren't home. During the school year, I would do my homework right after school so I could get back to the nearby schoolyard to play as quickly as possible.

Those nights filled with friends and cousins were wonderful times. But we weren't just physically close. Our whole family was also emotionally close — and we still are.

With the Mediterranean Sea only 10 minutes away from our apartment, the summers were truly magical. We went to the beach every weekend – and many weekdays as well – with my parents' friends and their children, or my uncle, aunts, and cousins. I loved the feeling of eating fresh, cold fruit while walking on the hot sand. I loved being held in the water by my father or Moshe and trying to catch the tiny fish that came close to shore. And I loved the way my father would hold me on his lap and wash my feet with cool water to remove all the sand before putting my shoes back on for the walk home.

Israel was a modest place back then, and no one ate in restaurants often. But we did have one treat each week, and that was our weekend trip to the pizzeria. What fun that was! We would gather as many family members as were available, and go together into town to order the most exotic and delicious food we children had ever heard of. To add to the excitement, sometimes we would top off the evening with a soft drink or ice cream cone.

I also have wonderful memories of one of my most prized possessions from those years, the beautiful little bicycle my father bought for me. He would take me around the neighborhood, walking right beside me while challenging me to ride without the training wheels touching the ground. I will never forget his smile when I managed to do it for the first time! He kept working with me until I was 100 percent confident and then he removed the training wheels. I was just flying all around the neighborhood. Moshe and I must have ridden around those streets for hundreds of miles, riding around the same few streets over and over, but we didn't care. We were so happy.

More than once, my tire went flat and my father would take me down to the basement to fix it, teaching me, showing me how to use his tools. Eventually, I could do it myself—turning my bike upside down, taking the chain out and then the inside of the wheel, putting the tire into a pot of water to find the hole, and then putting on the appropriate material to seal it tight. Not only was my father proud of me, but I have to admit I was pretty proud myself — and popular with my friends, too. I became the "go to" guy whenever my friends had problems with their tires.

When he could, my father took us traveling all over Israel. We would often pile into the car and head out on day trips to the forest between Tel Aviv and Jerusalem. When we had more time, he took us on long trips to the Galilee in the north and Eilat on the Red Sea in the far south. Wherever we went, we cooked our food over an open fire, played games, listened to music, and danced. It was a simple and beautiful time, with magical memories for me — a truly heavenly childhood.

The only thing that kept my young life from being absolutely perfect was the fact that my father was often gone from home.

Although he had a civilian job in the Israeli aircraft industry, he was often gone at night working a second, or even a third job. Sometimes he would work with his brothers in their business delivering cooking gas to homes, or he would set up cable TV or deliver eggs for the farmers. He always did whatever he needed to do to support his family.

And, just like everyone else of appropriate age in Israel, my father could be called up to active military duty at a moment's notice. As a child, it seemed to me they called him constantly. All of a sudden he would be gone — and we couldn't know where they were sending him or when he would return. There was no email in those days, and I don't remember ever talking to him by phone when he was called up. I do remember visiting him one time at a base, though, where it was so wonderful to see him and feel his arms around me again.

I loved the excitement of touching the big machine guns — so different than playing with my toys—and jumping on the heavy tanks. But at the same time, I was very much aware of what those enormous weapons could do to my father, and that terrified me.

I missed him so badly during his times away that my whole little body just ached for his hug. Many days, and especially many nights, I worried that something would happen to him — my biggest fear — or that someone would break into our apartment and hurt us, and we would never see him again. After sunset, when I would watch TV before bed, I would always keep looking toward the door with the hope that he would be coming in.

Sometimes, my mother would give us a few hours warning that he was on his way home. I could barely sit still knowing I would see him that same day! But other times, he would just walk in the door in his army uniform as a complete surprise to all of us — loaded down with bags of food, chocolates, candies, waffles, fresh fruits, and his huge smile.

"*Abba! Abba!*" I would jump in his arms, and squeeze him like I would never let go. When my father was back home with us, I had everything I could possibly want or need. My little world was complete.

On the other hand, as much as I hated him leaving for military missions, I was certainly very proud of the fact that the army needed my father's help. We boys in the neighborhood would brag to each other incessantly about our fathers' strength, but I knew my father was the strongest. I would ask him over and over again to show me his muscles and let me feel them. I never got tired of that game. No wonder the military called him away from us so often. That's how strong and special he was!

"You should see my father's muscles! They're gigantic," I would say to my friends. "He's so strong he can lift me up with just one arm!" And the other boys would chime in with claims of their own. In our free time, we boys watched Bruce Lee movies over and over again, always trying to figure out how we, too, could grow up to be as strong as Bruce Lee — and our fathers.

Underlying all our games was the awareness that we had to become strong because our country was at risk, always living at the cusp of war, if not in war directly. Many times I would open the world atlas just to look at the size of Israel, so small, and the surrounding countries — Jordan, Syria, Egypt — so very much bigger. It always scared me.

No wonder Israel needed my family to help protect us. Everyone knew my mother's family was so strong and brave after everything they went through to come to Israel, and my father — well, he was the best soldier in the land. A friend who had served in my father's unit during his initial active-duty service told us this story many times.

On this particular mission, the unit was sent to protect the Israeli border from Egyptians who had crossed into Israel. One night, there was a great deal of gunfire back and forth until only one Egyptian soldier was left standing. My father's entire unit was looking all over for this one man, but no one could find him. No matter where they shot, he always shot back.

My father and his friend were lying on the ground behind a bush when my father suddenly whispered that he thought he saw the enemy soldier. But it was so dark, he couldn't be sure. His friend encouraged him to take a shot; give it a try. So my father took one shot and then . . . quiet. They waited a while to be sure and then went to find him. Strapped to the dead soldier's back were many more weapons. My father had stopped this man before he could get farther into Israel and hurt many more people. I could not have been more proud.

. . .

It was a very sad and lonely time when our father was in the hospital. My mother sat with him all day and slept there every night; she never again went back to her job at the mall store. I'm sure she must have come home at some point to shower and change clothes, but I remember seeing her only rarely. Our nearby relatives and close friends also spent all their time at the hospital supporting my parents. In addition, they also dropped off food at our house every day.

And still, the three of us children did not know what had happened to our father. Our imaginations went wild, because no one would tell us a thing. I became more and more fearful that I would never see him again. There was rarely a moment that my stomach wasn't churning, that my heart felt relaxed.

The one person who stayed with the three of us children during that terrible time was my Aunt Leah, my mother's sister from Los Angeles. We had visited her and my uncle in the States a few years earlier, and they came often to Israel, so we knew her well and our families were very close.

But tragedy struck both sisters the same week. My Aunt Leah's husband died just the day before my father went into the hospital. Just when my mother was running out of my sister's school because something terrible had happened to her husband, my Aunt Leah was already on a plane to Israel with her husband's body in the cargo hold, to bury him in the holy land. At the very beginning of the grief that would engulf her — and at a time when she thought she would be turning to *us* for comfort and support — my Aunt Leah quickly buried her husband and turned her attention to caring for her niece and nephews. I do not know how she did it.

A lot of my sister's friends came to the house in those first few days after my father entered the hospital. But before long, they went back to their own teenage lives — including the girl Pazit considered her best friend — and my sister rarely saw them outside of school. That's when Pazit started pretending that everything was all right, everything was normal. After all, if nothing bad was happening, then she didn't have to feel so awful. I think that attitude worked for her for a while.

At school, the counselors suggested she try to calm herself by imagining she was at the beach.

"As soon as they said that, I started skipping school and going straight to the beach," Pazit told me later. "Why should I imagine that I'm at the beach when I can actually be there?"

I still played with my friends outside after school some days, but my heart wasn't in it. Every now and then, one of the boys would ask where my father was.

"He's in the hospital."

"Why? What happened?" Sometimes I would tell them the painful truth — that I knew he had been in an accident, but I didn't know what kind. Other times, I would just run home to my room. Looking back, I assume that most of my friends had heard about my father's accident from their own parents, probably with more details than I knew at that point. But they wouldn't tell me anything. None of them would.

Why didn't I know what was happening with my own father?

I know now that my mother didn't want to worry us any more than necessary and honestly did not know what to say. Would my father live? She didn't know. What should she tell us about the pain he was in? She didn't know that, either. She did what she thought was best for us, always.

While I certainly understand that now, at the time I worried incessantly that my father might never come home. For a sensitive, fearful child whose father was his world, it was a very dark and painful time. I spent a lot of my energy just trying to keep from crying.

I remember one night in particular when one of my parents' friends and their son came over to visit Aunt Leah and us, and we all watched an Israeli movie on TV. The story was about a divorced couple. Their child lived with the mother, who was a horrible person, and the wealthy stepfather. The child's father was a poor man, but he loved his child so much. The mother tried to kidnap the son and take him to Europe, but at the very last minute, the father ran through the airport and grabbed his son just before they got on the plane. They hugged him so tightly, just like I wanted to hug my father. I'll never forget how hard I worked to keep my tears inside at that moment, using every muscle in my body so I wouldn't embarrass myself. Looking back now, I wish I had allowed my tears to flow. I certainly had every reason to cry.

I have no idea how I sat through school during those weeks. I honestly don't remember a thing about it — except that my teachers were so kind and wonderful. They were like angels to me.

But the principal of our school was another matter.

One day a friend and I were late coming back to class from a break. All of a sudden, I felt a sting on my neck. The principal had grabbed each of us by the neck so fiercely, one in each hand, that her fingernails cut our necks and we were both bleeding. She dragged us into her office and literally threw each of us into a corner. My head hit the wall with such force that everyone could hear the "boom" throughout the room.

I was a good student. What had I done to deserve this treatment? I could feel the anger and humiliation just boiling inside me.

The next time I saw my mother, I told her what happened. I showed her the cuts on my neck and the bruise on my forehead. I wanted her to go up to the school to talk to the principal. Or better yet, to scream at her in front of everyone. Or even better, I wanted my mother to dig her fingernails into the principal's neck and see how *she* liked it.

My mother gently looked at my bruised head and the cuts on my neck, and she listened carefully to my whole sad tale. Then she said, "Jacob, what your principal did was wrong. And I'm so sorry she treated you like that. But I need you to understand that I cannot do anything about this right now. I just can't. I need to be with your father. You understand that, don't you? You are just going to have to handle this on your own."

Yes, I did understand. Of course I did. Because no matter what I was going through, no matter how badly I had been treated, I cared about my father more. Nothing else mattered more to me.

But the fact is that I went back to school a changed student.

Until that moment, I had always been so good in school, a good boy all around. I did what I was told and I did my best — for myself and for my parents, who had always let me know how important my education was from the time I was a very little boy.

I remember one day when I was first learning to write the alphabet. My father sat with me while I was painstakingly worked on my letters. The whole family was getting ready to go to a friend's house, but I was slow and hadn't finished yet.

"You go ahead, and we'll catch up," my father said to the rest of the family. "I'll stay here with Jacob while he finishes." And then he turned to me and said, "You take your time and work carefully, Jacob. It's not easy to learn to write the alphabet. But it's important to get it right." He sat with me so patiently until I finished, and he let me know how proud he was.

I had always felt the pull of my parents' desire for me to do well in school and their emphasis on my education. I was always friendly and smiling with my teachers. And I was smart; sometimes I would do Pazit's math homework for her, even though I was five years younger! But the incident with my principal pulled on me as well. I could not allow myself to be physically hurt and humiliated and just go on as if nothing wrong had happened. My 10-year-old self firmly believed that the principal owed me and my friend an apology; she had committed a grave injustice against us. I still believe it today. That was no way to treat a child, or anyone else.

Consequently, I went back to school an angry, uncaring student. I was filled with rage at my principal and a system that would allow her to injure a student like she did. I would show her. She wanted bad, I would give her bad. Her authority would mean nothing to me.

From that moment through my high-school graduation, I did everything I could to prove that I was as strong and tough and bad as any principal could ever be. I barely studied, I skipped school at every chance, and I was in trouble all the time.

Such a shame and a waste! I wish some teacher or counselor would have asked me what was really going on with me. Maybe I could have become the student I had been before that mistreatment. But no one ever did.

. . .

Finally, after more than two weeks of separation from my father — although it seemed infinitely long to me at the time — my mother came home one night to tell us we could visit him in the hospital the next morning.

"I will take you to see him tomorrow, and you'll be able to talk to him," she said. "But you cannot touch him. He is still very, very sick. So the hugs will have to wait for another time."

That's when she told us in very general terms about the car accident that had almost killed my father. We learned the full details of the story little by little — through the next weeks, months, and even years.

What we know now is that my father's assignment that day required him and two co-workers to work in a location away from the factory. They set out on the highway with my father driving a blue GMC Sonoma owned by the factory. One co-worker sat next to him in the passenger seat, and the other was in the back. Everything seemed absolutely normal.

And then, without warning of any kind, the entire front of the car exploded into shrapnel.

My father remembered wanting to pull over to the side of the road, but the steering wheel was in pieces. He remembered trying to stop the car, but the brakes wouldn't work. He also remembered screaming, "Help me! Help me!" But his co-worker in the back seat had jumped out, and the man in the passenger seat was in shock. Even if he could hear my father, he wasn't able to move.

My father knew immediately he was in very bad shape. One piece of shrapnel had almost severed his leg at the knee, and he was bleeding profusely. Another piece of shrapnel cut his right hand almost completely through; just one strand of muscle connected the pieces of his flesh. Another piece of metal had gone through his left hand with such force that it had broken every bone.

The car came to a stop on its own about one-half mile from the explosion site. Acting purely on instinct from his military training, my father threw himself on the floor. Then he ripped his shirt to create a tourniquet for his leg. His hands were so badly mangled that, to this day, I have no idea how he accomplished that. But had he not put the tourniquet on his leg, he surely would have bled to death before the ambulance arrived. And if he had stopped for even one second to look closely at his hands, he wouldn't have attempted the tourniquet. Really, it was a miracle. He lost consciousness in the ambulance, but he was alive.

Two of our relatives worked at the hospital where my father was taken, and they immediately called the aircraft factory and my uncles' business, so my Uncle Joseph drove to Pazit's school to get my mother right away. As soon as she saw Uncle Joseph running toward her down the school hallway, she started screaming.

"What happened? What happened?"

"There's been an accident, Sarah. That's all I know," he said. "Let's go."

Uncle Joseph drove my mother to the hospital, but it was difficult to get close to my father's room because the hallways were packed with people. My mother thought a member of parliament must have been injured in the same accident as my father, or maybe someone famous had had a heart attack. But those people had all come for my father — friends, relatives, and also coworkers and others my mother had never met. That's how many people loved my father.

When my mother and uncle finally pushed their way past the crowds, the doctor came out to see them.

"What happened? What happened?" My mother was crying.

"Your husband was in a very bad car accident, Mrs. Kimchy. We are doing everything we can to save his life. We're doing everything." And that was all he had time for. He went back into the room to work on my father.

But a few hours later, he came out again, clearly distraught.

"Mrs. Kimchy, I am so very sorry," he said to my mother. "We've done everything we know how to do. But your husband's injuries are so severe, there is just no way he can survive them. I am so sorry."

He told everyone who had gathered that it was time to go in and say goodbye to my father. But my uncles wouldn't hear of it. One of my uncles asked the doctor if he was sure my father would die.

"Yes, I'm afraid so," the doctor said. "I'm so very sorry."

"Has his heart stopped?" my uncle asked.

"Not yet," the doctor answered. "You still have time to say goodbye."

"But if his heart is still beating, then what the hell are you doing out here in the hall talking to us? Why aren't you in there working on him?"

"Mr. Kimchy, there is just nothing more we can do."

"Of course not — because you're out here in the hall talking to us! You get back in there and keep working on him. You do *everything* you can. You don't know Rami Kimchy. He is a fighter," my uncle said to this doctor. "You do not mention death again to us unless his heart has already stopped! Do you understand?"

The doctor went back into the room. He and his team worked on my father nonstop. A few days later, my father was stable, and my mother could go in and sit with him. It felt like a miracle.

My father's right leg had been amputated at the knee — although he would eventually require two additional surgeries that removed the leg almost up to the hip. But his right hand was still in question. The doctor asked for permission to amputate. He said the hand was just too badly mangled to save.

Again, my uncles said no.

"I really don't think you understand how badly damaged your brother's hand is," the doctor told them. "Even if we could somehow save it — and I don't believe we can — there is very little chance that he would ever be able to use it."

"You still don't know your patient," one of my uncles answered. "If there is even a slight chance — even the very, very slightest chance — that the hand could be usable again, Rami Kimchy will make it work. You will *not* amputate the hand."

And the hand was saved.

It was about 10 days after that decision that my mother told us of the accident. And true to her word, she took us to the hospital the following morning.

I was excited and jumpy, with no idea what to expect. I walked with my mother through the long halls, but barely noticed anyone around me. Then, as I turned the corner into my father's room, an overpowering medicinal smell hit me as hard as a physical presence. I still remember it to this day. And there in the bed across the room was my father — my father with two legs.

At first, I felt so confused that I couldn't do anything but stare. Then I realized that his "right leg" was really just a line of little pillows. No one had told my father that we knew about the amputation. So he had made sure the nurse fixed him up in bed to look like he had two legs. He didn't want to scare us.

Although I had waited through so many lonely and painful days to be with my father, seeing him that morning felt like the end of the world to me. His face was so filled with pain. His hands were so horrible to look at — completely covered in huge bandages with big pieces of metal sticking out all over. Yes, I knew he would be in a hospital bed and I knew he would have only one leg. But I had expected him to be the father I had always known. Instead, as I looked at this man, I just kept thinking, "My poor *abba*. My poor *abba*. What did they do to you? What?" My heart hurt so badly for him.

Standing in front of him that day, I realized his friend had been right when he said my father was my angel to care for now. Nothing mattered more than for him to know how much I loved him.

"*Abba*, you don't have to pretend to us," I said to hm. "We know you have only one leg and we don't care. We love you just the same. We always will."

Everyone standing behind me started to cry and they all

left the room — even the doctors and nurses. At the time, I had no idea why they'd left. And I didn't care. Finally, it was just my father and me.

CHAPTER FOUR

My Father's Resilience

The happiest times of my childhood were the moments my father arrived home from his military missions. Since we never knew when to expect him, his homecoming was the surprise I anxiously awaited from the moment he left. I would imagine his footsteps on the stairs outside our apartment, his voice at the door, his strong arms as I jumped up, the warm smell of him as I buried my face in his neck. And the knowledge that, at least for a while, the five of us were together and safe with no worries. Nothing bad had happened. My father was home. Soon we would be outside playing basketball.

This is the homecoming I imagined over and over again when I thought about my father finally leaving the hospital. Yes, he would be missing a leg and would have trouble using his hands for a while. My mother told us it would take a long time for him to fully heal. But what was a "long time" to a young boy anxious to have his father back? A few weeks? A few months? In my 10-year-old mind, everything would be the same as before.

Three months after the accident, I was either at school or swim class when my father finally did come home from the hospital — and for that, I will always be grateful. Had I been at home, I'm sure I would have been waiting at the window of our apartment. I would have rushed downstairs, anxious to get even a quick glimpse of my father, although my mother would have told me to stay out of the paramedics' way and let them do their work. My mother would have been anxious herself, as well as busy caring for Moshe, who broke his leg just the day before.

I would have seen them pull the stretcher out of the ambulance with my father on his back, looking up at the sky in front of the home he feared he might never see again. I would have seen them pulling and pushing him up the path to the front door of our building. And then, as the paramedics tried to negotiate the entryway — just the beginning of their journey up to our third-floor apartment in a building with no elevator — I would have seen Rami Kimchy fall to the ground.

I can only imagine the howling sounds that would have come from him, the screams from my mother, the apologies of the paramedics, the quick movements as they hurried to lift him back up to the stretcher. My father, my father! For this brave and noble man to have been dropped on the ground with no way to stop his fall — with thickly bandaged hands at the ends of arms he could barely move and the short stump of his right leg barely yet healed — it is almost more indignity and pain than I can bear for him. To this day, it breaks my heart to think of it.

But eventually, much more slowly and carefully, the paramedics climbed the stairs to our apartment. And when I did get home that day, my father was lying on the sofa in his own house — exactly where I knew he belonged. My heart could not have been happier.

Anyone else seeing my father on that couch, however —

anyone other than an adoring family member — would have been shocked, maybe even frightened, by the sight of him.

Both my father's hands were enormously swollen, and he could not move them. Every bone in his left hand had been broken, so the surgeon placed pins inside the bones — pins that then pierced the skin and came through to the outside. Even the thickest bandages that protected his hands did not cover the places where the pins exited the skin. They were always visible. And whenever the thick bandages were removed to be changed, we saw that both hands were completely covered by cuts and scars.

During those years, my friends and I often played with a popular plastic toy covered with seams that allowed the pieces to be turned and twisted. By twisting in specific ways, the toys could be changed from one form to another and back again. My father's hands, which I spent so much time staring at once he came home, looked exactly like those toys to me. His hands were so completely covered with lines from the surgeries, I felt I should be able to just twist the pieces and change them back into my father's "real hands" — fingers and hands and arms that could move in all directions with the full ability to feel what they were touching.

My father's mangled hands never frightened me. But for years to come, strangers would point and ask what had caused such scars, scars like they had never seen. Or not asking, they would simply stare and turn away. But to me, the sight of my father's hands always reminded me of his strength and determination during his long recuperation.

My father was completely focused on that recuperation from the moment he got home. The very next morning, the paramedics picked him up—never again dropping him—and took him to the hospital for hours of physical therapy, bringing him back weak and exhausted that night. And again the next day, and the next, and every day for the first month of the rehabilitation that would take years.

Millimeter by millimeter, my father regained some movement in his hands and arms, the whole family cheering him on with each slight improvement. If he could lift his arm a centimeter higher than the previous week, it was a cause for celebration. If we detected slight movement in his ring finger for the first time or a slightly tighter fist than he could make last month, we congratulated him as if he had moved a mountain — which as far as we were concerned, he had. For the rest of his life, my father never stopped working to improve the mobility and strength of his hands. He would never fully recover — never be able to feel the softness of his grandchildren's faces with all parts of his fingers, throw a basketball with much strength, grasp a pen as firmly as he would have liked, or continue his military service.

But eventually, his arms and hands would allow him to hug his children and grandchildren tightly, carry groceries, wash dishes, sign his name, and so many other activities he worked so hard to achieve, activities the rest of us take for granted every day.

The loss of his right leg was an even bigger challenge. Without the ability to walk, my father spent the first months of his recovery lying on the couch or in his bed between trips to the hospital, unable to do much of anything. After a while, he regained enough strength to move around our apartment in a wheelchair. About a year later, when his hands had mended well enough to bear weight and most of the pins were removed (some pins remained permanently), he learned to use crutches to hobble around. Several years after that, my father began to use a prosthetic leg, although he continued to need the crutches for balance. Eventually, he gained the confidence to walk with only one crutch. And only rarely did anyone ever again see Rami Kimchy feel strong and secure enough to walk on just two legs. I have very few such memories.

With all the physical and emotional pain of his recuperation, as he found himself dependent on the family he had once cared for in every way, I do not ever remember hearing my father complain or whine or curse his fate. Ever. He had been in an accident, and now he would face the rehabilitation. Period. He went about his life as if it were just that simple. His attitude made my father a heroic role model for his wife, children, siblings and, as it turned out, many strangers as well.

Each time my father went to physical therapy, he met other patients who also lost limbs. Many of these patients would talk to my father, crying and sharing that they wanted to end their lives because nothing would ever be the same as it was before. They couldn't see any way forward through the agony and the loss of mobility or dexterity. It was my father, carrying his own painful burdens, who encouraged them, told them they *could* make it through their physical therapy, and helped them see the many reasons to continue living. My father simply would not have known how to sit there and remain silent.

Helping other people had always been the essence of who he was. He was no different after the accident. I listened closely as my father would talk about his fellow patients and how he thought he might have helped this man or that woman just a bit. And I saw clearly that the more helpful he felt he had been, the stronger he seemed to become.

From my father's example, I learned one of the most important lessons of my life: Each of us has enough strength to give some of it to others. No matter how much pain we are in, we *always* become stronger by helping others become stronger.

A couple of years after the accident, we moved into a first-floor apartment with an elevator so my father wouldn't have to negotiate so many stairs with crutches. Now, he could go outside much more easily and had no worries if he wanted to visit neighbors living on another floor. Happily, one of my father's brothers moved into the same building with my aunt and four cousins. And with family so close by, I know my mother, in particular, felt more confident that my father would be able to get immediate help if he should need it. We were all so happy to be together.

But it was in our new apartment that I would hear my father scream out in the middle of the night, unable to contain himself against phantom pain, that malicious trick of the brain and spinal cord that affects so many amputees. No matter what, he would never take pain medication or go to the hospital to get help with pain, afraid of what the pills could lead to.

Awakened from a deep sleep, I would hear him crying out to God for help. With my heart pounding, I would run into my parents' room and jump into the bed, listening to my mother trying to calm him in any way she could. I don't remember how we first discovered this, but the only thing that seemed to help was for me to pound on the stump of his leg. For some reason, that seemed to relax him. He never called me to help him, and yet the minute I heard him in the night, I always came running.

I would pound and massage and talk to my father and pound some more. I remember speaking to the stump of his leg, begging it to stop hurting. In fact, I even gave his stump a name, calling it *Ze'era*, "little one." And then, as the pain would recede a bit and I could feel him start to relax, I would snuggle near him in the bed exhausted, and I would often fall asleep.

"Jacob," he would say to me later as he rubbed my back, "you can go back to bed. Jacob, thank you. Thank you." And I would go back to my bed, only to wake a few hours later for seventh grade, spending the day with classmates who could never imagine what I had been through while they slept.

I have always been grateful that I was able to help my father through those bad nights, in whatever way I could. Even as a child, I never wished I could have slept through his screams; I *wanted* to run to his side. Sharing those moments, being able to take away any tiny bit of his burden, brought my father and me even closer than we had ever been. And yet, as an adult, I now have to wonder what it must have been like for him to know that his screams and cries were waking his youngest child from a sound sleep. My poor father.

The phantom pain decreased over time, but even years later, it would attack him unexpectedly. About three years after the accident, we purchased a car specially fitted to be driven with the left leg, and my father had the freedom to once again leave the house on his own and drive around the city. Although with me around, he didn't have much opportunity to be alone! I went with my father every place I could, just for the chance to be near him. One day when I was a young teen, he had an attack of phantom pain while we were together in the car, completely stuck in traffic. As my father suddenly started screaming, I could feel the panic rise up in me.

"*Abba*, let's pull over, I'll help you!" But we were hemmed in by other cars with no way to even inch forward, much less pull over to the curb. As he screamed, my father started pounding on his leg to try to get it to relax. But nothing seemed to help.

"*Abba*, please! Let's leave the car here!" I told him. "Maybe you'll feel better if we walk. Let's get out of the car and find an ambulance."

But my father was in too much pain to even answer me.

So together we sat in that car, both of us hitting the stump of his leg, both of us screaming and probably crying, too, until finally the pain eased its grip just a bit. Seeing my father in that much pain right out in the middle of the city was one of the most helpless feelings of my life. I can't imagine what people in the cars next to us must have thought, although that was the last thing on my mind at the time.

While my father was thrilled to drive again, his real goal was to be able to run. He had no desire to run sprints or marathons; he had never been a runner. He just wanted to be able to move around like everyone else, and that included running down the street if he felt like it. Because he had such a tiny short stump, doctors did not have a lot to offer him in the way of prosthetic limbs. But there was one doctor in California who thought he could help.

Four years after the accident, we all went to Los Angeles for my father to be fitted with a prosthetic leg.

I had taken one other trip to the States with my family — to see my Aunt Leah and other relatives — but at 4 years old, I didn't remember much. This trip, on the other hand, was wonderful. My father was making good progress, we were all hopeful about a prosthetic leg, and it felt so good for all of us to be in such a new and exciting city with our American family. And of course, for a young teen, there just could not have been a "cooler" place than L.A.

My friends and I all knew what was "in" at that time — a brand of clothing called Quicksilver. But in Israel, if we could find it at all, it was too expensive. In L.A., however, the brand was relatively inexpensive, and we saw it everywhere. I told my parents that the only thing I wanted on the trip was to bring Quicksilver shirts back for my closest friends.

"Are you sure?" my mother asked. "You don't want anything else for yourself?"

"I'm sure," I told her.

"All right, if that's what you want. How many should we buy? Four? Five?"

I told her I needed 14 shirts for my fourteen closest friends. My mother must have been laughing to herself. What young teen has 14 closest friends? But she had said "yes," so my suitcase was stuffed with Quicksilver shirts two months later when my mother and we three kids flew home. I was thrilled to be able to make my friends so happy. And boy, did we think we were cool!

My father stayed behind in the States for several months to continue to work with the doctor and his new leg. It was a long, slow process of learning to walk all over again, using his hip muscles to propel his prosthetic leg forward. But my father kept at it, working as hard as he could every day. When he did come home, we were so proud. Although he never was able to run again — the U.S. doctor had been overly optimistic about that — my father was able to walk, sharing strolls in the neighborhood with my mother again, and we were so happy for them both.

It had taken more than four years to get there, but with the elevator, the freedom to drive, and his new prosthetic leg, my father had attained a level of mobility and independence he had feared he would never enjoy again.

Watching my father's own struggles and meeting so many other people who had lost limbs — listening to their stories, learning what they had been through, hearing about their loss and pain — changed me. I had always been a sensitive child, but I became even more so at about age 10: extremely sensitive and attuned to people who needed help, support, or sympathy. I realized that even people who looked so strong on the outside could be suffering on the inside. And it was clear to me that it was up to us to open our hearts to them. It was almost as if I were listening for the needs of others, ready to jump in and help at a moment's notice. At that time in my life, I believe I wanted to become a superhero.

I suddenly found that I wanted to help everyone — the first, of course, being my father. I wanted to be his guard, his protector, to be able to save his life if he needed me to. To do that, I knew I had to become very tough and resilient. I was swimming, going to the gym, and running and playing soccer in the neighborhood with my friends almost every day. My body became so strong and I worked to be as healthy as possible, always with the vision in my mind of my father as an old man and me next to him, lifting him, carrying him, helping him with everything he needed. I'm sure my friends saw the change in me then, too. But the irony is that just as I became rougher and tougher on the outside, I was becoming more and more sensitive on the inside.

My father had told me so many times to always remember that the sky was the limit, and this is when I started to believe it for myself.

. . .

We were constantly plagued by questions during my father's long recuperation: What had caused this accident? How can a car just explode into shrapnel? How is it that three co-workers could arrive for work in the morning, set out for a job site in a government car, and one of them has his life forever changed while the other two remain relatively unscathed? And the question I struggled with the most: Why did this have to happen to my father?

If my father himself ever asked "Why me?" none of us

heard him. He never complained about the accident and never seemed angry about it. He just went about the business of doing everything he could to recuperate, for the sake of his family as well as himself.

This placid attitude might be difficult for some people to understand, but it fit perfectly with his character. My father never showed anger about anything. In the whole of his life, I never once heard my father scream in anger or yell or even raise his voice to another human being. He was very simply the most peaceful and loveliest of people, soft and supportive to every person he knew and every stranger he met. Even in the most extreme circumstances, anger was just not in his nature.

I don't remember being angry about the accident, either. What I do remember is the deep and hollow sadness I felt, a sadness that in some ways has never completely left. I hurt for my father, for this strong and brave man to suffer so much physical pain and the small indignities, as well — the plastic chair he had to use because he could no longer stand while showering, the way he hopped around on one leg when he only had to cross a short distance, the way people made fun of his hands, the times that stepping on the smallest of pebbles could cause him to fall. But while I might not have been angry, I was well aware that many of the adults around me were quite angry and frustrated — my mother most especially — because they could not get a straight-forward answer to the most basic question: What had caused this car to explode?

We all saw the pictures taken after the accident. No one could believe someone could survive such damage. The engine, which in that car was located very near the driver's legs, had been blown through the cabin wall practically into the driver's seat. It was terrifying to see the sharp pieces of metal everywhere, the steering wheel in pieces. But by far the most upsetting aspect of the pictures to me was the blood all over the floor. That was my father's blood. Every time I saw the pictures, the sight of his blood sent a physical shock through my body.

The car was a government car, belonging to the Israeli aircraft industry, specifically to the largest factory in Israel at that time. Because a comprehensive file with mileage logs, maintenance records, and documentation of repairs was kept for every government car, my family felt sure the car's paperwork would reveal the cause of the accident. So we waited and we waited.

And then we were told the file didn't exist.

Yes, we were told, there was a file kept for each and every car. That was correct. But no, there was no file on this *particular* car. The government did not know one single thing about the vehicle that had shattered into my father's body that day. There were no records of mileage or usage, no history of maintenance, no history of repairs. There was nothing. The only information the factory would reveal was the fact that yes, it was its car. No other facts were available.

My parents turned to the police for help. But the police confirmed the government's story: there was simply no information available about this car. None. And for reasons they never shared with my family, the police chose to not investigate further. No matter what we tried, no matter whom we spoke to, no matter who did the asking, we were never successful in getting any information at all about that car.

Eventually, experts from GMC America came to Israel. After inspecting the car, studying the photos, and talking with representatives of the Israeli aircraft industry, GMC America, determined that the accident had been caused by an explosion in the clutch.

No one among our family and friends had ever heard of such a thing — even those who were very familiar with automobile engineering. In fact, my father's accident was the first and only such explosion ever recorded.

GMC accused the factory of using a substandard part in the car, which the factory vehemently denied. But who was right? How could either side support its position if no maintenance records were available? And why would an aircraft factory use a substandard part in one of its own cars? There were no answers.

Did my parents ask all the right questions? Did they push hard enough in all the right places for answers? Probably not. They were absolutely overwhelmed at the time, my father with the pain of his injuries and my mother with caring for my father and the three of us. They just did not have the energy.

As a child, I heard the information we were given at the time and never questioned it. They told us the clutch had exploded, so that was my story. But as I got older, I asked my mother many times what she really thought had happened. We never reached any conclusion.

Twenty-seven years later, the questions still bother me. So much so, in fact, that I recently contacted GMC America. I emailed the appropriate individual and explained the history and all the information I had about the accident. I asked several specific questions. And then I waited for the personal response that never came.

Instead, I received a form letter by email telling me to contact a different department. But I never did. And I won't. I do not want to spend any more of my energy fighting for answers that will never come.

I have accepted that my family will never know the full truth.

. . .

When you are injured in Israel and unable to work, the National Health Insurance gives you a stipend for the rest of your life, the amount of which depends on the severity of your injury. The amount the state offered my father was too low for my parents to consider, so they sued for a more fair compensation. The lawsuit dragged on for years, the state waiting until my father had his prosthetic leg so they could say he hadn't been "crippled" by the accident, hiring detectives to document all the things my father *could* do but completely ignoring his struggles. My father knew National Health Insurance investigators were following him and photographing everything he did. The detectives even rented an apartment in the building next door to ours with their living room facing our living room! Finally, my father hid in our doorway on the street downstairs to surprise them one day, revealing himself when they came home to their own apartment door.

"Do you want to take my picture?" he asked them in the nicest voice. "Go ahead. You don't have to sneak around, pretending you're not following me. You have my permission. What would you like to know?" I have no idea how they answered.

One day, the National Health Insurance office called our house, and my mother answered the phone.

"Mrs. Kimchy, we need to talk to you about your husband's prosthetic leg," the woman said. "He uses a special pad every time he puts the leg on. I want you to know that we found a cheaper supplier for those pads, one that will charge us 50 cents less per pad. This is the one you will use from now on." Unlike my father, my mother certainly knew how to raise her voice in anger and she did not waste any time. She hung up the phone, ran out the front door with her car keys, and drove straight over to the insurance office.

"Where's the doctor who made the decision that my husband would use a cheaper pad?" she yelled at the woman who had been on the phone with her. "I need to talk to him right now. Right now!"

"There's no doctor here in this office, Mrs. Kimchy."

That stopped my mother for a second. "Are you telling me that someone other than a medical doctor made the decision to take away the pad that is the best for my husband?"

The woman had to admit that was the case.

"Have you ever met my husband? Has anyone here ever met my husband?" They had not. "Then how dare you tell me what I can and cannot do to keep him comfortable! Do you realize how little he's asking? How dare you!"

The insurance office agreed to my mother's demand; my father would continue to use the highest quality pads, the ones that cost the state an additional $3.50 per week.

Time after time, my mother felt beaten down by the National Health Insurance office. She fought with them constantly. My father's body was almost destroyed in the accident, and more than once, my mother said she felt the state was trying to destroy his soul, as well — trying to prove that he was fine, that the state didn't owe him much because he was as good as new. My father had fought in every war for this country, had left his family to serve on additional missions every time they asked. And this is how they treated him in return? My father might have handled it all with his uniquely placid attitude. But my mother, understandably, was angry enough for the both of them.

Finally, five years after the accident, the State of Israel and Rami Kimchy agreed to a settlement. Neither side was completely satisfied with the result, but my father knew his family would be cared for.

CHAPTER FIVE

Untouchable

During the years my family was primarily focused on my father's accident and recuperation, the rest of the world — certainly including Israel — continued with its own problems, problems I was more or less successful in ignoring.

Just a few months after my father's accident, the Intifada (which later we would call the First Intifada) began. As a child suffering such trauma in his own family, the reports of Palestinian demonstrations and violence were just background noise in my life. Nothing touched me directly, nothing could have impacted my world as much as my father's accident. I do remember hearing family members discuss politics as my father recuperated. However, with no Internet or cell phones and only one television in the house, I just didn't hear the news very often. I was certainly glad my father was not involved in dangerous military missions. But whatever I heard about the Intifada, it did not seem to be directly connected to my life.

That all changed in 1991 when the outside world brought its problems directly into our home.

With the First Intifada still underway, Saddam Hussein Invaded Kuwait and claimed it as an Iraqi province. The world condemned the action, but Hussein had no intention of leaving Kuwait. Instead, he used Israel as a pawn, threatening to send missiles with chemical warheads into Israel if any country dared to use force against Iraq. Israelis took him at his word. We couldn't afford not to.

And so months before the U.S. coalition began bombarding Iraq in what we now call the First Gulf War, we began preparing to defend ourselves. The Israeli government told us how to make our homes safe from gases that could be released by chemical weapons. We were assigned to various government distribution points to get vaccinated and pick up our gas masks. I watched my father hop around the apartment on one leg trying to get everything ready, putting up the special plastic we were told to glue over our windows, going with my mother to shop for enough food and water to last several months for seven people -- the five of us plus my father's parents who lived nearby. It was an inspiration to watch this man take care of everything to protect his family, even though he was just learning how to live life again himself. We helped with everything, preparing as best as we could, while still trying to go about our normal lives.

Then, in mid-January 1991, the U.S. and coalition countries began bombing Iraq with the goal of forcing its withdrawal from Kuwait. The very next day, Iraq began launching Scud missiles into Israel, toward Tel Aviv, near our home, and Haifa.

We stayed indoors, as the government instructed. All schools were closed throughout the country, as were almost all offices and factories. For one month, we lived in the dark with all our doors and curtains shut and just the tiniest bit of light coming in from the balcony. Thankfully, Saddam Hussein did not send the chemical weapons he had claimed to have. But his missiles could kill with or without chemical warheads, and they terrified us.

Not surprisingly, after a few weeks being cooped up in the house, I begged and begged my mother to allow me to go out — just across the street to see my friend Yonit. Finally, I wore my mother down. She agreed to let me go on the conditions that I take my gas mask with me and would run home immediately if I heard the air-raid siren. I kissed my parents and joyfully ran with my mask right across the street into Yonit's building. Even though her apartment, too, was dark and dismal, it felt so good to be somewhere new.

But before too long, the sirens started. I ran to the front door.

"Jacob, where are you going? Put your mask on!" Yonit's parents were screaming at me. "Come into the safe room now!"

"I have to go home."

"Don't go out there! You could get hit! Jacob!"

But I ran outside clutching my gas mask.

As soon as the door closed behind me, I could feel the blast of the air-raid siren throughout my whole body. The sound was absolutely terrifying. Time seemed to slow down. I looked left and then right and realized I was the only person in the street. As if I were in a dream, every step I took seemed to stretch time out even further. The siren told me the missile was on its way right that second. I wondered if I would live through the interminable few steps it would take for me to get home. Where would it land? Would it land on my street? On me? Anything was possible. I was physically shaking so hard, that it took me several tries to open the front door to our building, even using both hands. Not waiting for the elevator, I ran up the several flights of steps to our apartment.

"Hurry! Hurry!" My mother was screaming for me as soon as she heard me at the door. "Let's go! Now!"

We all rushed together into the safe room. We heard the

hideous thud of the missile hitting the ground not far from us, as we had heard it so many times before. It took a long time for my heart to calm down that day as I prayed to God that my family would be safe.

We were lucky; the missiles never hit anyone in our family. The attack ended after one month. We eventually put our gas masks away, opened our windows, and ventured out into the streets. Adults went back to work, children went back to school, and our lives continued on. But none of us ever forgot the screaming of the air-raid sirens or the sickening sound of the missiles hitting the ground.

. . .

If there was one constant in my life during my father's hospitalization and recuperation, other than my constant anxiety about his health, it was this: I swam. And I swam.

My parents had belonged to a country club, and my father had taken me with him to the club just before my father's accident at the beginning of fifth grade. He asked if I wanted to learn how to swim. I loved playing in the water at the ocean's edge and jumping over the smallest waves. But I didn't know how to swim, and I was embarrassed to look at all the kids swimming past me in the pool so fast.

"I am not sure it's for me, *Abba*," I told him. "I really don't think I can make it."

"That's OK, Jacob," my father said. "But look how much fun the other children are having. I really think you'd like it, too. I promise I'll hold you in my arms the whole time until you tell me it's OK to let go."

I agreed. Once I got in and relaxed a bit, I realized he was right. It *was* fun, and I paddled around a bit. So when my father asked me again if I wanted to learn how to swim, I said I thought I would. Before I could change my mind, my father called the swim coach right over to us and told him I wanted to sign up for classes.

"All right. Jacob, I'm going to test you out with the four main swimming strokes so I can see what you know," the swim coach said. "Are you ready?"

"OK." I had no idea what he was talking about. When he finished the test, he announced he would put me in "basic."

A couple of months later, I was still in "basic." I was also taking trumpet lessons at the time, and enjoyed both activities. But to get to the trumpet lessons, I had to cross a major street, and after my father's accident, my mother became terrified I would be hit by a car. She arranged for a taxi to take me back and forth to swim class several times a week — in fact, I don't think I missed one class — but asked me to give up the music lessons. If I had to keep only one activity, I was glad it was swimming for one simple reason: the coach's daughter.

Even at age 10, I knew a beautiful girl when I saw one. I could have watched her for hours gliding through the pool, turning at the wall, pushing off with such force. I was mesmerized.

She might have been the reason I was anxious to get to swim class, but once I started training, I discovered my own strength. Pushing myself harder and harder, lap after lap, my anxieties about my father and my hatred of school and the injustices of the world seemed to fall away. I found I could lose myself in the repetition of the strokes, the rhythmic sounds of my own exhalations under the water. I pushed and pushed until I thought my lungs would burst, until I could barely climb into the taxi when it came to take me home. Swimming became a calming, almost meditative experience for me. That exhaustion brought me a sense of peace I found in few other places during the early months and the years of my father's recuperation.

My coach was a kind man who had a lot of empathy for my family situation. But he also recognized my natural talent long before I did, and I became his favorite. He would ask me to demonstrate the skills, telling the others to watch my arms or legs and pay attention to my technique. Before long, I received the medal for "most improved" swimmer.

It was also through swimming that I began to recognize and develop my competitive nature. My father's accident had left me with a feeling of powerlessness, but as a swimmer I had an "enemy" to beat — whether it was own time, my own distance, or the swimmer in the next lane. I found that I could push myself beyond what I thought was possible, even beyond what my coach demanded of me. And I almost always won.

When I was one level below the competition team, my coach had a dilemma. He could send only one swimmer to the team, but we had two top swimmers who were almost evenly matched. One was myself. The other had a brother on the competition team and he, of course, wanted to join his brother on that team. This boy came up to me one night after class.

"Let's go, right now, you and me, one on one for the top spot. You see this here?" He was holding a plastic cup in his hand and he made sure I saw that he was crushing it to pieces. "This is what I'll do to you in the water, Kimchy. Right now, you and me!"

My coach heard his challenge and motioned toward the pool with his head. "Get on the springboards. Two laps. Let's see who wins."

I swam my heart out that afternoon, giving it every single thing I had, but I lost by one second. Nevertheless, I knew I had done my best and I was satisfied. When I got out of the pool, the other swimmer reached out his hand to shake mine.

"Wow, you really are a great swimmer," he said. "Congratulations."

To my surprise, the coach picked me to join the competition team. A few weeks later, I competed along with all the top swimmers in Israel. I was 12 years old when I became the Israeli national champion in the butterfly stroke — not in my own age group, but in the age group above me. I was an absolute fish. In the water, there was nothing I could not do, bringing home five or six medals from every swim meet, so excited to show them to my parents, so eager to see the way my father's eyes lit up with pride.

I felt absolutely invincible in the water — until the day when stabbing pains in my ears caused me to double over in agony.

My mother took me to a doctor who said my ears had become sensitive to the water. He suggested I stop swimming. If I didn't, he warned, I risked permanent hearing loss. But I was a champion, and any hearing loss was far off in a future I could barely imagine. What importance was my future health compared to the power I felt in the water, the joy of bringing my newest medals home to my father? I kept swimming.

My parents accepted my decision and continued to support my training in every way they could — paying for taxi after taxi, buying the best special ear plugs and swimming cap, paying for me to go to the gym with my team, holding dinner, praising my many accomplishments — everything except the one thing I wished for most: I wanted them to *be there*. They were never at poolside, never in the stands cheering me on.

I understood, of course. Even as my father's recuperation progressed, it was just too risky for him to come to the pool — too slippery, too dangerous for a man who was learning to walk all over again. And my mother needed to be with my father. Of course I understood. But that didn't make me any less sad. I was always alone, while the other boys' parents would be right there with them, even jogging alongside lap after lap.

"You can do it! Push harder! Keep going! Be strong!"

Through every practice and at every competition, I heard them screaming for their children — helping my competitors, sharing their strength. It was very difficult for me. Every athlete needs that unique emotional support that can come only from family. So as I swam and heard everyone else's parents cheering for them, I stayed focused on my one goal: to bring another medal home to my father. After swim meets, I would climb into the bus that was provided for swimmers who didn't have any other ride home. I would watch everyone else get into the cars with their parents. I was the champion, and that did feel great. But I was so lonely on those long rides home.

My ear pain continued to worsen, with one ear infection after the next. At age 14, when we went to the States to get my father's prosthetic leg, the pain was so intense that I started screaming on the plane. No one knew what to do for me. I couldn't calm myself down.

When we got back home, I wanted to keep swimming. But there were times I was in so much pain that I just couldn't make it to the pool and I found myself having to take long periods off to let my ears heal. Like any athlete, when I stopped training for weeks at a time, I stopped progressing. My skills suffered so much in fact that I eventually found myself dead last in a race, barely able to finish. I was absolutely humiliated.

My coach told me to step back to a lower-level team, and my doctor ordered me to stop swimming. The time had come. I stopped swimming at age 16.

It was so very difficult for me to willingly give up an activity that had once been a source of such confidence, that had helped sustain me during one of the most painful periods of my life. But I soon found a new interest in my life, one that helped take my mind off swimming. I had a girlfriend.

I had noticed Ayelet at the main gate of the school in the mornings. She was a sophomore, the skinny short girl everyone wanted to be with, and I was a junior. We would talk in the mornings before school and before long, we were inseparable. If teenagers are really lucky, they have a special spark with that first love, and we had it all. We lived close to each other, our families were close, and we shared absolutely everything together. In the winter, we would sometimes wear one sweater together — the two of us walking around in it as if we were one person, which is exactly how our relationship seemed to me.

Only with Ayelet could I be my true self. She was the only person with whom I shared the pain I held so tightly inside, the constant sadness and worry about my father. Ayelet was the only one who knew of the terror I felt when I saw a car that reminded me of the accident, the panic that would flood my body as every muscle tightened and I braced myself against the explosion that never came, so sure that the unsuspecting driver was about to be injured or killed. She was the only one who knew of the panic I felt each time I heard an ambulance siren.

"Jacob, just think about this," she would say as she gently rubbed my back. "That siren is probably taking a woman to the hospital to have her baby. It's OK. You don't have to worry." And it helped, a bit.

I worked so hard to act strong and to *be* strong for my family and friends, and I will always be grateful to have had this special, fully accepting love at such a crucial time in my young life.

Of course, our time together wasn't always so serious. As girlfriend and boyfriend, we also had a lot of wonderful, normal teenage fun with each other and with our friends. And although we eventually each went our separate ways, we remain close friends to this day.

In school during those years, I worked very hard to do as little as possible. When I was in class, I spent most of my time sitting in the back of the room sketching and re-sketching the MTV logo. But truthfully, I tried to stay out of school as much as possible. We were supposed to come early for extra classes twice a week, which I never did. And I skipped out every other chance I got as well, going to the beach or the flea markets and always finding other students there, too. We weren't "bad kids." We didn't do drugs, we didn't steal or cause problems for people. We just didn't go to school.

I might have looked like a tough guy on the outside — at least I hoped I did! — but for me, my desire to avoid school started out to be all about fear. I never forgot that feeling of my head hitting the wall when I was thrown into the corner in fifth grade, stunned. It terrified me. Beginning in seventh grade and continuing for three years, I had a teacher who constantly screamed and berated her students every day. When that teacher called home to complain that I was skipping school and my mother asked me to explain myself, I told her the truth about how horrible this woman was to everyone and how all the students were afraid of her. My mother went up to school to talk to the teacher, but nothing changed.

Every now and then in fifth and sixth grades, a student

would tease me about my father. "Your father only has one leg! I bet he's such a weakling, he can't do anything!" Of course I would start throwing punches as fast and as hard as I could.

By high school, I just did not care about school at all — and I got into fights just for the thrill of it and to show how tough I was. After one fight, I was expelled for three days. I was thrilled. What a great vacation for me!

But despite my best efforts to avoid anything to do with school, I eventually found myself in an extraordinary learning situation that changed my life in many ways. My high school matched me up with a 7-year-old boy who needed tutoring. This boy lived in a poverty-stricken high-crime area, and even the bus ride to his home frightened me. When I got off the bus, I saw a neighborhood filled with boarded-up buildings, the type of urban decay I had previously only seen in movies. A few students in my school came from this community, and based on their stories, I was greatly relieved that I wasn't attacked between the bus and the boy's house. But even inside his house, I didn't feel safe. It was small and very dark. The boy's mother and older brother were at home, but no one welcomed me or said anything to me at all. Looking back now, I think the whole family was just numb from living in such poverty. But at the time, all I felt was fear.

And yet, I didn't back out of the project. Twice a month for that whole school year, I fought my fear and took the bus to this boy's house. We would work on his homework together, look through his notebooks, and study a bit, although I wasn't sure how much he really understood. We would kick the ball around and ride bikes together. But most importantly, we would talk. I'm not sure how many friends this boy had, friends who really understood his situation. I knew what it was like to feel different, to have things on your mind that your classmates couldn't understand, and I wanted this little boy to know he could talk to me.

I wish I could say I made a huge difference in his life, but I honestly don't know that that's true. What I do know is that I made *some* difference, letting him know that he could trust me and that I cared enough to keep coming back to help him. I made sure to let him know he was important to me.

That tutoring was a crucial experience for me — my first taste of helping someone outside my family, my first opportunity to realize how much I had to give, how right and good it felt to make a difference in someone else's life, and a new perspective on my own middle-class life.

Several years later, I took an opportunity to mentor another student, this one a young teen whose family had recently emigrated from Russia. His father was in the hospital for cancer treatments, and his mother was busy caring for his father — a situation I could certainly relate to. The boy's Hebrew wasn't yet perfect, and he felt completely separated from other students his age. So in addition to working on homework together, I became his friend. I would take him to the field to play soccer, specifically so the other kids would see him with an older friend. We would meet with another tutor-student couple in Tel Aviv to play video games, and we spent many hours just talking.

I learned so much from this boy. When I saw him trying so hard to be cool and how fearful he was of not being good enough, I recognized those same feelings within myself. After my father's accident, so much of the happiness and confidence I had about myself and about my life in general had just evaporated. For a few years, I had been absolutely lost. I worried about my father's physical pain, about the dangers he faced every single day just trying to walk down the street, about the sadness he must have felt to no longer be working and "useful." I worried when I saw people pointing and whispering behind his back. I worried when my parents were upset about the lawsuit and the benefits they had to fight so hard for.

I had lost a part of my strength and no longer felt I measured up to the other kids. But I had not really seen that in myself until I saw it in this young boy. I became determined to help him develop a sense of his own strength, his own worth, to help him feel better about himself. And what a joy that was! I discovered again — as I had in my first tutoring experience — what a great pleasure it is to be there for another person, to help rebuild their soul, whatever the cause of their difficulties. Again, I realized that when I helped someone else become stronger, I became stronger, too.

I had yet another opportunity to learn that lesson by helping a group of children with various disabilities. These children were amazing, welcoming me right away with big hugs and open smiles, so happy to have another friend to play with. Once or twice a week, we would play basketball or some other games, and I would help them make their dinner. The more I got to know them, the more I saw their true abilities, and the less I noticed their limitations.

One night, sitting down to eat with them, I found myself directly across from a girl in a wheelchair. This particular girl, who had an aide with her at all times, couldn't speak, but she could mumble and she could certainly laugh. Right in the middle of dinner, she started laughing with food in her mouth — and she accidentally spit some of it out onto me. Maybe another volunteer would have handled it differently and tried to help her learn better table manners, but I immediately started laughing. The gleam in this girl's eye was just contagious. And taking their cue from me, everyone else started laughing, too.

For whatever reason — and I suspect it was my experience coping with my father's injuries — I was able to enjoy caring for people with a variety of special needs in ways that others couldn't. I didn't mind feeding people when necessary or helping them to the bathroom. I saw again the power I had to make other people happy, people who were different and isolated through no fault of their own. And, as always, I gained so much from these experiences -- as much as the people I was helping.

. . .

Like all Israelis, my processing into the military began when I was a junior in high school. The military checks your background, physical and mental health, intelligence, and physical strength to determine whether they will offer you a position in one of the seven special units such as intelligence, rescue, and commando. I received an invitation from all seven special units.

I will never forget the day I received the invitations. I was coming home with my group of friends, when I heard my mother calling me from our fifth-floor balcony.

"Jacob, you got the invitation to the Air Force! They want you to be a pilot!"

My father was standing next to her with a huge smile on his face, waving hello with both hands. I knew it was such a meaningful moment for them. But at the same time, I was so embarrassed in front of my friends — all of us always trying to be so tough — that I just screamed up to my mother that I'd be home soon!

When I did get home, I sat down with my parents who suggested I consider pilot training, or the commando unit (similar to the U.S. Navy Seals) because of my background in swimming. I knew there would be some time before I had to make a final decision, but I replied to the letter indicating an interest in those two units. I knew how happy and proud of me my parents were.

In March of my junior year of high school, the commando training began with a two-day session. One thousand students came from all over Israel, knowing the military would take only the top 10 percent into the unit. Other special units held their trainings on different days, with 1,000 students per each unit. We were all tested for physical strength and endurance that first day. I ranked third out of the 1,000 applicants, and I felt sure I would make it into the pilot or commando force. And yet, before the two-day session ended, I dropped out.

The truth was that I had never wanted to be in one of the special units; I had signed up to make my parents happy. And I knew the special units would spend much more time away from home — usually three or four weeks at a time — than regular military units. I just could not consider being away from my father for that long. Even taking three-*day* trips away from home was difficult for me in high school.

No one was very happy about my decision. My parents were very disappointed. And even Ayelet — who was so close to me and knew almost every secret in my heart — couldn't understand why I was skipping such a privilege that others could only wish for. But I just couldn't do it. I could not leave my parents' home for so long. On the outside, I was a strong guy with an invitation to join a special unit of the Israeli military. On the inside, I was a sensitive boy who could not imagine being so far from home, a child still wanting to hold his father's hand for security. And what if something happened to my father while I was gone? What if the phantom pain started again? What if he needed me?

I was embarrassed by my feelings and I never shared them with my friends. Even my family didn't know the full depth of my need to be with them. I know they sensed something. But the full truth was too painful, too difficult for me to talk about. So I left the special-unit training without any additional explanation and went home to receive my "regular" assignment.

After graduating from high school, I spent a month in the U.S. visiting family, and then began my three-year service in the Israeli military, starting in the Air Force. I went home as often as I possibly could during that time. Depending on my assignment and the specific situation in Israel at any given moment, I was often able get home twice a month for a quick visit. Those were such joyous and meaningful times for me — to check on my father's health, to be back with my family, to be a child again for even a day.

I had two other friends from Rishon Lezion in my unit, and we would try to coordinate our visits home. From where we were stationed in the north, we would take the train back down to the center of the country, laughing the whole way and often singing songs from children's TV shows at the top of our lungs. People think soldiers are grown men and women, but they're not. They're just kids who feel desperate to be away for a few minutes from the ever-stressful and often-terrifying business of protecting their country.

If I wasn't able to get home for a while, my parents would come visit me. They knew they wouldn't be allowed into the base, but they would spend hours on the road driving north just in the hope I could get away for a quick half-hour visit. Those painfully short visits were bittersweet for me, but I was always so appreciative that they had driven so far just for a quick few hugs. I thanked them incessantly and hated to see them go. I missed them terribly.

One day when I was home visiting, I was at the apartment with my mother while my father went out to run some errands. Awhile after he left, he called me.

"Jacob," he said. And I knew immediately from his voice that something was very wrong. "I've been in an accident. They're taking me to the hospital."

I started screaming hysterically to my mother, while my father was still on the phone.

"*Abba's* been in an accident! He's been in an accident!"

"Jacob, I'm OK," it was my father's voice. "I'm OK. Don't worry." He gave me the name of the intersection where the accident occurred, just two miles from our house.

"He's been in an accident! Let's go! Let's go!" No matter how fast my mother was moving, it wasn't fast enough for me.

I stayed on the phone, and my father tried to keep me calm while we ran to find him.

"Please don't worry so much, Jacob. Please. I'm really OK."

By the time we got there, the ambulance had come and my father was already wearing a neck brace. After just a few days of discomfort, he really was fine. But I was not. This small accident, medically nothing more than an inconvenience, raised all my fears and worries once again. I wouldn't say I had fully recovered emotionally from his accident 10 years earlier — never again would I be as carefree and positive about life as I had been before that day — but I had started to believe again that everything could be all right. I could see that my father was healthier, happier, and physically able to do all the activities that were most important to him. He and my mother traveled a lot, and they enjoyed themselves immensely

But it was all so fragile. One person could make one wrong move, hit my father's car, and the sirens would be screaming again, bringing my worst fears and worst nightmares back to life. This reminded me that my father, whose love and strength was absolutely crucial to my existence, was completely vulnerable. I planned to move back home just as soon as I finished my service.

In the third year of my service, a rumor started to circulate that a classmate of ours from home had been killed. We had no email or cell phones and very limited access to information, so several days passed before we learned the rumor was true. Ronen Eshel had been stationed on the far northern Israeli border with Lebanon. Terrorists using anti-tank missiles had killed Ronen and one other soldier. He was 21 years old, as was I.

Ronen and I had known each other since middle school when we played handball together. We were on the same volleyball team In high school, working hard together hours every day for months at a time. We were part of the same large group of friends who hung out together every chance we got. And now, it was impossible to believe he was gone. We had lost so many people in Israel from wars and terrorism, but losing Ronen brought our own mortality home in a way that nothing else had. We talked about him incessantly, about his life, his family, his death — trying our best to figure out what it all meant.

As soon as my required military stint was over in 1998, I moved right back into my parents' home in Rishon Lezion and prepared to enroll in the College of Management Academic Studies to study finance. Although I hadn't been any kind of student in high school, this was different. There hadn't been much I could do to protect my father when I was younger. But now, as an adult, I vowed that I would push myself as hard as I could. I planned to become a stock broker and open an investment firm. If my father ever needed me to take care of him financially, I would be ready.

CHAPTER SIX

Life on a Roll

Toward the end of my military service, my father decided it was time for him to go back to work. Almost 12 years out from his accident, he was feeling well, walking as securely as he ever would, and driving comfortably in a specially outfitted car. He was ready to be productive and feel useful again. So my father bought a taxi, a white Mercedes taxi — fairly common in Israel — and went into business for himself.

On my next visit home, he couldn't wait to take me for a ride. Boy, that car could move — and my father was so proud! It was so wonderful to see him happy and energized, waking up in the morning knowing he would be doing something meaningful to contribute to the family and community. In fact, he had planned to work only a few hours each day, but he loved the taxi so much that his workdays slowly became longer and longer.

Before starting college, I took a job working nights at a gas station — part of a program for soldiers who had finished their duty, in which the government offered bonuses for taking jobs that were difficult to fill. Every single night, my father would come to bring me dinner and buy gas.

"Hey, *you*," he would say in front of everyone with a big smile, "can you please fill my taxi with gasoline?" And every night he would tip me, making sure other customers could see. My father was just so cute, this little man driving up in his big taxi! This became our nighttime ritual, a ritual we both loved.

It was also around this time that my sister had her first child. When my nephew smiled, my father's face absolutely lit up. He appreciated every second with this little boy, as if he had lived his whole life just for this very moment. I had never seen him happier. In fact, now with his grandson and his taxi business, my father proclaimed himself the happiest person in the world.

I began my college studies in the fall of 1998. I was committed and serious about my schoolwork, and I did well. But my father was concerned that our house was not a good place for me to study. We had some very noisy neighbors, and one day, my father asked one of them to please keep the noise down. In response, the man pushed my father to the ground.

My father never told my brother, Moshe, or me about this episode. He knew we would never allow anyone to push — or even touch — our father in anger. If we had known about it when it happened, we would have made it sure it would have been the last time that neighbor ever even looked at our father. When I finally heard about the incident from my mother, I was furious. What kind of a person pushes a man to the ground — a sweet man with only one leg, no less — because he asks you to keep your music turned down to a reasonable level?

"*Abba!* You have to go to the police! You have to report this man. He can't get away with this," I told him. "Believe me, I'm happy to tell him directly what I think of what he did! But if you don't want me to do that, please at least report him to the police."

But that was not my father's way, and I knew that before I even spoke to him.

"Jacob, think about it. What would that accomplish? Yes, he pushed me. But he's our neighbor, and we have to get along. No police for me," he said. "But I am concerned about how you can study with all that loud music."

So, my father gave me my own renovated, furnished four-bedroom apartment.

"You have to have a quiet place to study. And this way you can rent out the other rooms to students and make some money," he reasoned.

Any student in my position would have been thrilled. So I moved in, and I have to admit I really enjoyed myself. How many students are fortunate enough for their parents to completely pay for their education and to pay for an apartment, too — when they could just as easily have lived at home? And if that weren't enough, my father visited me every day with bags and baskets of food. Here was this middle-aged man with his awkward gait and scarred hands that still gave him problems, carrying bags of food to *me*, a perfectly healthy young man. My father was a hero like that. And if that weren't enough, he gave me a beautiful sports car with all the extras! My life was more than perfect. No one could have asked for more.

But after a few months, I decided to move back home.

"What's the matter with you? Are you crazy?" Moshe, who lived at home with my parents, couldn't believe my choice. "*Abba* is paying for you to have your own apartment, all the privacy in the world. You can party every night if you want to — and you want to move back in here with us? What a sucker. What is wrong with you?"

Maybe Moshe was right and something *was* wrong with me. Maybe it wasn't normal for a young man to want to live with his family instead of enjoying the freedom everyone else seemed to crave. But I could never escape my desire to spend as much time with my parents as possible. After all those childhood nights running to my father's bed in response to his screams, helping in whatever way I could, I was always afraid that my father might need me and I wouldn't be there to help him.

My friends, who had helped me move in just a few months, earlier came again to help me move out. I gave the key to the apartment back to my father. But I continued to drive the sports car.

At the end of my freshman year, I approached my father with a proposition: Suppose I took a year off college and spent that year at a computer school to become certified in computer programming — with the promise that I would go back to college immediately afterward to finish my bachelor's degree. This was the "dot.com" era, and the importance of learning to build and manage websites and start up new Internet-based businesses was clear to me. But since my father was paying my tuition, he was the boss. He agreed with my plan and supported me in every way. I enrolled in the computer school and took a part-time job managing a video store.

. . .

Life in my little world felt wonderful and secure compared to what my family had been though years earlier.

Not only was my father becoming stronger and stronger, but my own life was absolutely overflowing with excitement — friends old and new, business ideas, plans for the future, lots of girls to date. And I felt I had learned so much about relationships from my first girlfriend that I was ready to meet "the one" and to give her my heart.

In programming school, when we were assigned to build our first website, I studied day and night, reading, learning, and memorizing everything I possibly could. In its short history, the modern state of Israel had become known as a startup nation, a place of constant innovation and reinvention. And within that framework, I set my sites to become the first big startup guy of the "dot.com" era. I received tremendous feedback on my work from my teacher. Forming a group with a few talented classmates, we started to build our dreams and set our sights on new targets.

My life felt just perfect. In fact, I was so happy that my friends nicknamed me "Smiley." Family and friends said they could just see the great energy coming out of my eyes, my physical smile, and my words. I felt unstoppable, and I knew I could become anything and everything I wanted.

But outside the walls of my own wonderful existence, life had become much more frightening.

I hadn't been particularly aware of the news during the First Intifada, which had occurred during the first few years after my father's accident and ended when I was a teenager. But now things were different: I had grown up and changed my perspective, and the world had changed, too.

"Terrorism" was a word now constantly on our lips.

I hadn't yet started college the very first time I personally knew people affected by terrorism. It was the night before the Jewish holiday of Purim, and the streets were filled with people celebrating in costume. A suicide bomber blew himself up in a busy intersection adjacent to the Dizengoff Center, the largest shopping mall in Tel Aviv, killing 13 people and wounding 130. Two of those hurt in the attack were friends of mine. Our focus was on our friends — who, thankfully, recovered quickly from their wounds — and we saw the attack itself as an isolated incident. We couldn't foresee that the violence would erupt over and over again, eventually becoming the Second Intifada two years later.

By 2000, every time we heard of an attack — whether it was a shooting in a restaurant or a suicide bomber anywhere in Israel — my friends and I would call each other in a panic. Those of us who grew up together in our little neighborhood of Rishon Lezion were now living all over the country, whether for college, work, or a military career, and we needed that tangible reassurance that our friends and families were all right.

But as the Second Intifada grew, the attacks came closer and closer to our lives. During the year I studied at the computer school, some friends and I had dinner one night in Herzliya, just north of Tel Aviv. Two days later, that restaurant was attacked by terrorists who parked a car bomb just outside. A suicide bomber blew himself up at a coffee shop in Jerusalem just the day after I had been there.

One summer night at a friend's house, waiting for him to get ready to go into Tel Aviv for some fun, I turned on his TV to find horrific images of a suicide bombing — 21 young people murdered at a beachfront dance club in Tel Aviv. We never went out that night. Instead, we spent the evening glued to the TV, sick with the knowledge that the bodies being removed from the club could easily have been our own.

For a while, there was an attack every day. The constant news and the fear of violence was so painful, so sad, that it went into every person's blood and into every person's soul. It seemed that every night we watched the same images on TV — the police and firefighters screaming as they climbed across piles of debris that used to be a shopping mall or a café or an office building, trying to find any survivors and get them to hospitals as quickly as possible. Crowds of people crying and shrieking and searching for loved ones. And always the same final images — bodies being carried away in a slow procession of ambulances with no reason to hurry. Every night, the news pierced our hearts. No matter where we tried to turn our minds, we could not escape the constant fear, the constant horrific images of death.

One Tuesday afternoon in 2001, my father called me just as I was coming out of class.

"Jacob, can you come home now?" he asked. It was an unusual request in the middle of the day.

"What's going on? *Abba*, are you OK?"

"Have you heard?"

"Heard what? I've been in class. What?"

I could feel my heart start to race. Was my father all right? What had happened to him?

"Jacob, come home now. Please."

I got home as fast as I could. It was September 11.

We stared at the TV and cried together as if we were losing our own family, as if this tragedy had happened in our own neighborhood — because that's how it felt. It was too much to believe; and yet the feelings were completely familiar. The fear on people's faces and the screams, the images of people running to escape the cloud of flying glass and shrapnel, people jumping from buildings. All Israelis felt such a strong connection to America, our greatest ally. But for my family, it was more than that. Part of our family lived in the States, and I had just been to New York City a few months earlier to meet with potential investors for a project. Once again, I couldn't avoid the realization that it could have been me. It could have been any of us.

"This is a terrible thing. But the buildings will stand. The people inside will be rescued, you'll see," my father said as we wiped our eyes. "Those buildings will not come down."

But as we sat together in front of the TV for the rest of

the day, we watched with the rest of the world as the buildings did come down, as thousands of innocent people were murdered right before our eyes in an instant. What had these people done to deserve such a fate? We cried because it seemed there was nothing else we could do.

CHAPTER SEVEN

The Unimaginable

A few months later, the panic of this relentless violence landed directly on my doorstep when I received a call from a college friend who worked in Israeli Intelligence. She was the one who kept all of us posted on attacks, starting the phone tree to check on our circle of friends. But this time she was screaming.

"Jacob! Where are you? Are you at work? Are you at the video store?"

I wasn't.

"There's a terrorist. There's a terrorist in the shopping area right near the video store. Right now!" she said. She told me to have the employees close down the store.

I called the store with my heart pounding, my hands sweating as I punched the numbers on my phone. But when the employee answered, I tried to speak calmly. "Who's in the store?" I asked. "Is there anyone in the store you don't know? Anyone who isn't a regular customer?"

"No, no one. Only people we know."

"OK, listen carefully. Lock the doors now. Close the blinds. Get everyone into the bathroom and stay there." I thought my heart would jump out of my chest.

"Why? What's happening?" She started to cry. "Jacob, what's happening?" But she didn't need an answer; she knew.

I explained what I knew, keeping her on the phone while she closed down the store. I tried to keep my voice calm. But I knew that at any second, this young woman could be taking her last breath, the phone in her hand exploding into pieces. Eventually my friend from Intelligence called in: The police had caught the terrorist. The employee began sobbing in relief. I sobbed with her, my emotions of relief, fear, and anger all tied up together. The danger was over — for now, for this instant.

Toward the end of my sophomore year, this same friend from Israeli Intelligence called again. This time I was out with my friend Sasi at night after class.

"Jacob!" I heard my name, and then she screamed something I couldn't understand.

"Why are you yelling at me? Slow down, slow down."

"Listen to me! There's been a suicide bombing in Rishon Lezion!"

"What?"

"Yes! Just now. Are you there now? Where are you?"

"I'm out with a friend having a late dinner. Rishon Lezion?" What was she saying?

"Are you all right? Where *are* you?"

"Where?"

"Jacob! Go home. Please! Throw some money on the table, run to your car, and go home! There could be other bombs. I'm hanging up."

"No, no wait! Where is it? I want to go help the survivors."

She gave me the address. And then she asked in a more subdued voice, "Jacob, are you sure you're willing to be a witness to this crime?"

I was sure.

All my military training propelled me to run *toward* the scene, to run to help. All the carnage we saw on TV night after night, always wishing I could do something to help—this time I would help. We ran to the car, and Sasi started driving straight toward the attack. We didn't recognize the specific address, but we knew what section of the city to head toward. This time, the bomb had not exploded at the other end of the country — this was our *home*. He drove faster and faster, while the realization descended on us that we could find a friend or family member injured or dead. Both Sasi and I were physically shaking from the fear and adrenaline coursing through our bodies.

Never in my life had I been so afraid.

I called my parents at home. No answer. Then I called my father's cell phone. It was disconnected.

And that is when everything stopped. Everything was suddenly completely still — even though I knew Sasi was driving faster and faster, running stop signs now.

"Sasi, my father got killed." I could hear myself speaking very slowly, in a daze. "In the attack just now. He was killed."

I felt a wave of ice move through my body, straight out from my heart.

Sasi glanced over at me as he tore through the town. "What are you talking about?"

"His phone isn't working. He got murdered today. I know it."

"Don't say that! Don't even think like that! Cell phones screw up all the time. You know that! Jacob, he'll be fine."

He drove even faster, his face now frozen, his mind now also in a daze. I called my father's number over and over. Nothing.

Just five days earlier I had seen my father's body in my dream, lying on a table, covered in white at his funeral. I had written a note the next morning to tell him how much I had loved him. I wondered now where that note was. I saw the buildings flying by. Was it in those jeans lying on the floor of my room? Sasi stared straight ahead. Had I put it in my desk? My mind wandered around my room to find the note, but I couldn't see it.

I called home again, but no answer. I reached my sister to check on her, my brother on his cell, and a few friends. The closer we got to the address of the bombing, the more crowded the streets became. Sasi let me out, and I ran toward the ambulances and fire trucks that were just starting to gather near the building.

The attack had been at the Sheffield Club, a café, pool hall, and one of the many places in Israel that everyone knew offered illegal gambling. But the Club, which had been on the third floor, was gone. Much of it had fallen into the second floor, where dark smoke poured out of a gaping hole. Some of it had exploded into the streets that were covered with glass and metal and other debris I didn't want to look at. People were coming down the stairs from the club covered with blood. Those of us who had come to help supported the victims who were able to walk to the ambulances. We picked up those who were lying in the street, hurrying, hurrying before it was too late for them.

Within minutes, the police and military drove up and poured into the streets — so many at once that it became difficult to move. The noise grew to a deafening pitch, but the scene felt completely silent to me at the same time. I became disoriented by the physical chaos. I felt as if I were on a movie set, as if the "extras" were playing a scene about a terrorist attack and I had wandered onto the wrong stage. Wasn't I just going to dinner with Sasi? I couldn't move for a few seconds, frozen in place by shock.

But this *was* my reality now. I pulled myself back from extraneous thoughts, forcing myself to remember that I had come to this scene not only to help whomever I could, but also to bear witness to this attack for my whole country, for everyone who could not see this directly, for all of humanity. It fell on my shoulders to expose the truth, and I could not do that unless I paid attention to every detail and recorded it inside myself.

I forced my way through the crowd and started up the staircase that led to the club. I had a strong, terrifying feeling that my father's body would be facing me at the top of the stairs. But truthfully, I was also terrified that I might find my father alive in there — in pain again, bleeding again, screaming again. What would my poor father have to go through this time? What? What if he had lost his other leg? What if he had lost an arm, or both arms? How would he survive this time? What would this sensitive man be facing this time? I had such a strong feeling my father was in there. Countless terrifying scenarios ran through my mind as I went up those stairs, my heart banging around wildly inside my chest.

But nothing — not my most horrifying nightmares — could have prepared me for what I found.

I stepped onto a slippery floor that was covered in red as if the ceiling had been raining blood. The room was filled with mismatched fingers and feet, a leg here, a head over in the corner, three arms resting near a pile of twisted metal. A man's body was draped across what was left of the club's big picture window. Impaled on the remaining glass, he hung half in the room, half out over the street. Black smoke poured out around him.

I suddenly remembered hearing astronauts describe the feeling of blasting off into space: being physically lifted out of normal reality, hearts pounding, skin sweating, every piece of their beings shaking, completely enveloped by a level of noise they had never imagined. That's how I felt in what was left of the Sheffield Club that night — as if I were being pushed up into an alternate reality, into some other world, while my heart pounded and pounded inside a body that couldn't stop shaking.

And who did those fingers and legs belong to? Men who had stopped in to relax after a long day at work. Teenagers who had come with friends for a game of pool. What had these people done to deserve being pulled apart limb from limb?

"Get out! Get out!"

Through the dizzying roar in my head, I recognized the screams of policemen.

"Get out! There could be another bomb!"

"I'm here to help!"

"Get out!" They pushed me out of the room along with all the other civilians who had come to help.

I went back down the stairs, my feet slipping and covered in blood. As my foot reached the sidewalk, I looked up. Directly in front of me was a white Mercedes taxi turned crosswise to the street, every window blown out.

It was his. It was my father's white taxi.

One moment I was standing and the next I had collapsed to the ground. I lay on the concrete with the glass shards and the metal and blood, feeling I would never move or breathe again, my brain jumping from place to place, not knowing where to turn. But maybe it wasn't his taxi. Maybe a different child had just lost his father, not me. With a tremendous effort, I pushed myself up from the ground to look at the number on the taxi.

It was his.

I pulled out my phone. After a few rings, my mother answered.

"*Ima*, have you heard what happened?"

"What? I was asleep. Why are you calling so late?"

"Turn on the TV, *Ima*. There was a bombing in town," I said.

"What?"

"Where's *Abba?*"

"He's working," she answered.

"No. *Abba* was murdered."

"What are you talking about? I said he's in town working!"

"Call your family in L.A. now. Tell them to come for the funeral! And please, call the family here."

"Jacob, what's the matter with you?"

"*Ima*, I'm looking at *Abba's* taxi right now, right in front of the bombing. The building is totally destroyed. *Abba's* phone is dead."

"What?"

"*Ima*, what's his license plate number? Tell it to me."

As she said every number, my eyes moved to the next, hoping for a mismatch. But every single digit matched my father's plate exactly. I told her I would call her back as soon as I had more information, and I hung up the phone. I knew my poor mother would be in shock and would feel panicked. But I couldn't worry right then. I had to find my father.

I called my friend at Intelligence trying to get more information. When she answered, I was talking so fast and loud she could hardly understand me. I told her about finding his taxi outside the club and my fear that he was murdered.

"What? What are you saying? I can't understand!"

"Just please try to find out anything you can about Rami Kimchy. Call me back as soon as you know anything."

As soon as we hung up, I called another friend who worked at City Hall. This girl knew my father very well.

"Just give me the names of the injured and the dead. That's all I'm asking for." But she didn't have the list yet. She promised to call me back as soon as she received any details.

I tried to go back into the building to look for my father, just in case. But the police pushed me out and into the street.

"I think my *abba* is in there! I have to find him!"

"No one's in there!"

I would get past them for a few seconds, and they would push me out again, more aggressively each time. I went back into the crowd and found some of my friends.

"My *abba's* been murdered! My *abba*!" I screamed to be heard above the chaos and told them about the taxi. They looked at me, but no one spoke, all of them shocked into silence by the total devastation.

At midnight, I called my mother again. This time she answered right away.

"*Ima*, what's going on? Who have you spoken to?"

"You tell *me* what's going on. I can't reach *Abba*."

"Of course you can't reach him! He got killed!" I was screaming as loud as I could over the wailing of the sirens and the crowds. "Did you call the family?"

"No. I'm not calling the family! Everything will be OK."

I found Sasi. I told him what I'd seen and shared my fears about my father. I asked him to drive me home. Although it was a short ride, it seemed to take forever; I couldn't wait to see my mother and make sure she was all right. When he pulled up to our building, I hugged Sasi and promised to update him as soon as I could.

When I walked into the apartment, my brother was there.

"Moshe . . . "

"I don't believe what you're trying to tell *Ima!* I don't believe it. What's happening? What's going on?"

I told him about the taxi, but he said he didn't believe me. I knew he couldn't *allow* himself to believe me.

"Then come see for yourself." I called my father's number again and again, but always nothing.

"*Ima*, we're going to the scene of the bombing," Moshe said. "We'll call you when we get there."

We hugged her. By this time, she was in front of the television, watching the breaking news.

I tried to drive him to the bombing site, but the police had closed off the whole area. I told Moshe I would wait in the car if he wanted to get out and see the taxi for himself. He left the car and ran toward the club.

In a few minutes, he was back. When he spoke, he didn't look at me. It was as if he were talking to himself. "I saw his car. But how can this be happening? I don't believe it."

Just then, we saw a long row of ambulances slowly leaving the scene in procession. We followed them, knowing they could be headed only one place: Abu Kabir.

Abu Kabir. These were the words all Israelis knew and dreaded, the syllables we heard over and over on the news every night. Another suicide bombing? Abu Kabir. An Israeli soldier found dead on the side of the road, stabbed by a terrorist? Abu Kabir. Occasionally, people would refer to it as a hospital. But if so, it was a hospital only for the dead.

Abu Kabir was the Tel Aviv forensic institute where the dead were identified and analyzed, where body parts were returned to those for whom a respectful burial of *something* was the most they could now hope for. This was where my brother and I went to find our father.

The news media arrived before us — knowing that whatever the details of this particular attack, the story would end at Abu Kabir. They asked us questions as we walked from the parking lot, but I pushed past them and headed straight toward the building. Moshe stopped to talk.

What was I doing? I kept asking myself over and over. Why was I at Abu Kabir? I wondered if I were in a nightmare — I *wanted* to be in a nightmare. But no, I fought against that wish. I had to stay alert, to see everything, to remember everything, to report everything for the sake of my people. Every second, I wanted to lie down and give up in tears. But I forced myself to pay attention.

And now, I saw myself walking through the doors into Abu Kabir. A group of social workers, called in at the news of the attack, were in the hallway — preparing to face the families at the worst moment in their lives. I was one of the first to arrive.

"Why are you here?" one of the social workers came forward to ask me.

"Because my *abba* was involved in the attack."

The social worker had asked and heard these same lines so many times, the familiar formalities of life in a country infected with the disease of terrorism.

I told her Moshe had stopped to talk to the press. When he joined us, she took us into a small room, asking questions and helping us fill out forms. But after checking the records, she told us no one named Rami Kimchy had been brought in.

"You don't understand," I told her. "I have to find my *abba*."

"But I just don't think he's here."

As I argued with her, I began to feel the tiniest sliver of hope. What if the social worker was right and my father had not been brought to Abu Kabir? What if he had parked his taxi and walked down the street to get a coffee just before the bombing? What if his phone had been incinerated in the blast, but *he* was somewhere safe? But I allowed myself to hold onto that thought only for a second. I knew my father would have reached us by now, more than an hour after the bombing. I knew he would have found a phone somewhere. He would have done whatever he had to do to let us know he was alive. He would not have allowed us to go through this torment. But maybe he was somewhere injured, too injured to use a phone. What if he needed me and I couldn't find him?

My mind ran in circles.

"There doesn't seem to be anyone here by that name, but tell me what your father looks like."

"Gray hair, blue eyes, 5 feet, 10 inches."

"And what was he wearing today?"

"What was he wearing?" I shook my head. "I don't know."

Moshe didn't know either. The social worker asked if we could find out.

I called my mother, but she couldn't remember his clothes.

"Think, *Ima*. What was he wearing? Please. What did he wear today?" But she couldn't remember.

"Is there anything else you can tell me that might help us recognize him?" the social worker asked.

I shook my head. My mind felt cloudy, I couldn't think. But then I realized they could recognize him by his prosthetic leg. "And he has pins in both hands—from surgery."

"All right. That helps. If your father gets here, we'll know who he is." She told us to sit in the hall and wait.

I called my mother again. My phone had very little battery left, and I knew I would need to call her many more times that night. So each conversation was very short, even curt. She was home alone, and I worried about telling her too much too quickly. I was afraid she could have a heart attack or a stroke from the shock. But I didn't have enough phone battery to talk to her slowly and calmly, to keep her on the phone while we both tried to understand what was happening. Just a few words of information was all I could give.

At about 1:30 in the morning, people started flooding into the building. The hallways became packed with chaos — people screaming, yelling at the staff, yelling into their phones, crying into each other's necks. I wanted to cry so badly that I felt my chest would explode, but no tears would come. Moshe and I just sat there. We didn't say much. We didn't even look at each other. Our heads were filled with the sights and sounds of what we had just witnessed, and every inch of our bodies was filled with the fear of losing our father.

I'm not sure what time it was when we saw one of my father's brothers, also named Moshe, walking toward us from the end of the hall.

Uncle Moshe had gone to all the nearby hospitals looking for my father — but nothing. In desperation, he had come to Abu Kabir. Walking in, he might have had some pocket of hope still in his heart. But when he saw us, his face contorted with pain.

"Dear God, wasn't it enough already? Why Rami?" he screamed. "Why?"

He cried with a piercing sob I had never heard before in my life. My brother and I hugged him and told him we should all hope for the best. But he seemed completely destroyed. Uncle Moshe was such a strong man, like my father, and I had always seen him as such a tough character and strong personality. Now, he was crashing down in front of me. I didn't know what to do. People all through the hallways were crying and screaming in ways I had never heard. The sadness choked all of us until it was almost impossible to breathe. I remember wondering how these social workers could have taken on a job like this.

Like the other families there that night, the three of us huddled together in the hallway for several more hours, waiting and waiting until I felt I couldn't take one more minute. I ran down the hallway and out the back door of the building, pushing everyone aside. Finally alone in an empty field behind Abu Kabir, I cried like I had never cried in my life. My tears, my screams — I felt as if my whole life were pouring out of me into the dirt. I don't know how long I stayed there.

When I finally walked slowly back into the building, I realized that my brother and uncle were gone. I immediately assumed they had been taken to meet with the person who delivers the final answers to the families. I was terrified, terrified to hear the news from which there is no way back. I sat on the bench to wait for the most painful truth I would ever hear in my life. I sat alone for a few minutes with my head down. Then I started looking for my brother or uncle, or the social worker who had spoken to us originally. And there she was — headed toward me. I had never felt my heart beat so fast in my life. Even if I had wanted to speak with her, I wouldn't have been able to.

"Kimchy, come with me," she said. "You need to join your brother and your uncle."

I followed her on a short walk to the room where we found them. I had wanted those steps to take forever, but there we were. We entered a small room where my uncle lay on the floor crying. My brother was standing, but his face was perfectly white with no expression at all. And there was one more person in the room. I recognized the head of Abu Kabir, a doctor we saw on the news almost every night.

My brother, Moshe, spoke first.

"Jacob, we don't have a father any more. We lost *Abba* today."

I looked at the doctor.

"It's true. You've lost your father. I'm so sorry to tell you that."

This moment could not be happening. I felt like I was high up on a cloud, wanting to wake up from a dream. I wanted to scream, to cry, I wanted to hug my father. But I took a breath and made sure to stay very calm and focused on the outside.

"I need to see him."

"No," the doctor said. "That's not possible."

"I need to see his body."

"I wish you could," he said to me. "But I can't help you with that."

"Look, I realize the body is in very bad shape. I was at the scene and I understand. But he's my *abba*. And you've just told me that he's dead. I need to see his body!"

"I am so sorry." The doctor shook his head. "But there's nothing for you to see."

"We're talking about my *abba!* I have to see him! Let me at least look at his eyes. I want to say goodbye to him."

"Jacob, please listen to me. You should remember your father as he was. There is nothing for you to see."

"You keep saying that! Why do you keep saying it?"

The doctor spoke quietly and slowly, looking directly at me. "You told us he had a prosthetic leg. We did find a few very specific pieces of metal at the site that could only have come from a prosthetic leg." He stopped for a moment. "But there was no body attached to it."

"What?"

"There was no body. The body was gone."

"Gone?"

"Yes."

No one moved. We listened to my uncle cry.

"I don't care if you tell me his body is wrecked and

crushed and burned — I don't care! I have to see him!"

"Jacob, I know it is hard for you to hear this. I know it's hard for you to understand this right now. But there is nothing left of your father's body. I am so sorry, but it's true."

I looked at my brother and my uncle, then looked again at the doctor and said, "I understand you're trying to protect me from seeing him in such a horrible condition," I said. "But I am asking you, please, let me just see his eyes."

The doctor looked at me and said slowly once again, "Jacob, there is nothing left of his body for you to see."

I tried hard to understand, to make sense of what he was telling me. It was impossible for me to leave without seeing my father. What was he telling me? I just couldn't understand his words. I couldn't accept them. I continued to ask him again and again to show me my father, in whatever condition he was in. I promised him I could handle it, no matter what. But he continued to tell me there was nothing left of my father for me to see. Eventually, I stopped asking.

"Now," the doctor took a deep breath and sighed, "which of you is the older brother?"

Moshe said he was.

"Then please, Moshe, I need you to go into the next room. The police have some papers for you to sign."

He signed. Date of death: May 7, 2002.

We didn't know what to do next. We stood there.

"Take these papers with you and go home," the doctor said. "You will be going home to a different life now. I am sorry."

We helped my uncle up, and the three of us walked outside toward our cars, through groups of terrified families waiting to hear the same words we had just heard. We didn't say a word. We couldn't.

Once my brother and I were in the car, I asked him to

call mom and tell her the news.

"I can't call her, Jacob. Please. You do it."

"I can't. I can't do it. You signed the papers, Moshe. You need to tell her."

"Please. Please do it. You've already talked to her tonight. She's expecting your voice. Please."

"Moshe, I can't. I can't do this."

Earlier in the evening, I had told my mother that our father had died. Moshe was right about that. But those calls were based on my feelings and my fears. Now that we *knew*, how could we say the words that would bring such unbearable pain to our mother? How do you tell someone you love that her husband has been murdered? Moshe and I went back and forth, on and on, neither of us wanting to do it.

In the end, I made the call. She answered right away.

"*Ima*, it's done," I said softly. "*Abba* is not with us anymore. We've just left Abu Kabir."

She was silent.

"Just try to relax, *Ima*." I kept my voice as calm as I could. "Moshe and I are on our way. We'll be there soon."

She hung up the phone.

The sun was rising as we pulled into the garage. We opened the door of the apartment to the screams and cries of those who had already come to mourn with our mother.

CHAPTER EIGHT

Lost

Within hours, the house was filled with hundreds of people.

I was exhausted, but we had too much to do to think about sleeping—and for that, I was grateful. I couldn't face the thought of lying down right then, couldn't face being alone with the images in my head. I called a few of my close friends, starting with Sasi. He had seen the bombing site and knew the chance of my father surviving was slim. But still, it was different to hear the finality of it, and it hit him very hard. At first I wasn't sure he had heard me. And then he spoke in a low voice, "Oh, Jacob. I am so sorry. Be strong. I'll be there soon."

As I called several other friends, I realized some of them had already heard the news. All of them told me they would be over right away. Some of them took several days off work to spend as much time with us as they possibly could.

My mother asked one of our cousins to go to my father's taxi to look for any personal effects. We didn't want to lose whatever physical pieces we might be able to find — pens my father might have used, papers he had scribbled notes on, anything at all that would give us back any tiny, tiny piece of him.

A woman walked up to my cousin as he tried to open one of the car doors. The door was stuck, so he reached over the broken window to try the latch from the inside.

"Is this your taxi?" she asked. She seemed distressed. "Do you know the driver?"

"Yes. The driver was my Uncle Rami Kimchy." He turned to face the woman. "He was murdered in the attack last night."

"Oh, no." The woman looked down at the ground and shook her head.

"One attack after the next," my cousin said. "Another life and another and another. What are they doing to us?"

"But this one . . ."

"Fifteen people killed. That's what we've heard so far. My Uncle Rami was such a good man. There could not have been a better man."

"It's my fault," she said.

"What did you say?"

"I said it's my fault." She looked up at my cousin. "Your uncle was in the Sheffield Club last night because of me. He wouldn't have been in there. I made him go."

The woman explained that she had been my father's passenger the previous night. The plan was for my father to pick up another passenger at the Sheffield Club.

"But she never came down. I was so tired, and I just wanted to go already. So I finally asked the driver to go in and see what was taking her so long. And he did." She looked up at what was left of the building. "And then this. The driver. . ."

My cousin stared at the building, then looked back at the woman. "Were you waiting here for us all night?"

"I thought someone might come. I had to tell you. You don't know how sorry I am."

"We appreciate that," he told her. "But you need to go home. This wasn't your fault. You know that, right? It wasn't your fault."

She shook her head. "I sent him there."

My family never heard from this woman again. We never knew her name or whether she was a regular customer of my father's. But she gave us something so valuable that morning. She helped me see my father that night, to picture what he had done and why: A passenger had asked for his help, so he went. It was as simple as that.

No one in my family ever blamed this woman for my father's death, not for a minute. Immediately after the blast, Hamas had used the Hezbollah television channel to claim responsibility for the attack. This woman had not sent my father to his death. Hamas had.

We learned that the murderer was a teenage boy who detonated his bomb soon after walking into the club. His youth didn't surprise us. Most suicide bombers were brainwashed 17-, 18-, or 19-year-old boys blowing themselves to bits with approval from their parents, who were usually paid by Hamas after the attack. The people who helped plan the attack — outfitting the teen with the bomb and a suitcase full of metal fragments and bolts to maximize casualties, and transporting him to the Sheffield Club — were arrested by Israeli Intelligence and later imprisoned. These same individuals had masterminded several bombings, killing more than 35 people all together.

But the single most disturbing fact about my father's murder was something I learned many years later from one of the survivors: The bomber had been standing directly next to my father when he yelled "Allahu Akbar!" Did he realize what was happening to him when he heard that? We were all familiar with those Arabic words — the words meaning

"God is greater" or "God is greatest" — that terrorists would yell just before an attack. They had been reported in the news over and over. What must my father have felt, facing his own death in that second or half-second? It breaks my heart again and again to think about it. No human being should ever have to die like that.

The day after the murder, I went to my college to update them about what had happened and to let them know I wouldn't be coming in during the shiva, the period when family and friends come to comfort Jewish mourners. I had very little time because I needed to get back to help my family, so I parked my car and ran into my program office to speak to the secretary.

"I'm not sure if you know already, but my father was murdered last night at the attack in Rishon Lezion," I told her. Everyone in the room looked at me in silence. They didn't need to say a word; I knew where their hearts were. The secretary gave me her condolences and a hug.

"You take your time and don't rush," she said. "We'll be here when things are easier for you. In the meantime, I'll update the dean."

I thanked her and ran back to the parking garage. As I drove toward the attendant at the exit gate, I realized I had no wallet or student identification with me.

"Look at the ticket and you'll see I was only here about 15 minutes," I told her. "I have no money and no ID with me. My father was murdered last night, and I just came to update the secretary of my program."

She looked at me and said, "I'm sorry. But you'll need to pay the money if you want to get your car out." I couldn't believe what I'd heard. I opened my door and stepped outside.

"My father was murdered last night!" I screamed. "I have no money with me. Open the gate!"

She looked at me, but the gate didn't budge. Just then I saw another person who worked in the garage come running toward me.

"I'm so sorry," she said. "So sorry." And she ordered the other worker to open the gate.

I thanked her and rushed home to begin my new life.

My Aunt Shoshana took care of the funeral arrangements, but we needed to get the word out to the community. I had seen funeral posters in my neighborhood since I was a child — plain white signs with black lettering to let everyone know the date, time, and location of a funeral. I knew what they were. But when my aunt handed me the posters and asked for my help, I just stared at them, not quite knowing what to do.

"Put them up in the neighborhood, Jacob. Please," she said. "We don't have much time."

"I know, but . . . ." I could only look at the posters and shake my head.

I asked two friends who were in the house to come with me.

"What am I doing?" I asked them as we walked outside. "Look at this. Am I putting up signs of my own father's funeral? The posters say Rami Kimchy. I can't believe I'm doing this."

I realize now I was in shock that day. I had learned of my father's murder, witnessed a scene of immeasurable violence, and not slept in 36 hours. My legs walked me through the neighborhood. My arms held the posters. My hands put them on walls and light posts. But my "self" seemed to be somewhere else entirely.

That day and the next, time became a physical force pulling me forward against my will, dragging my body and soul toward a moment I never wanted to reach — my father's funeral. How was this possible? How could I keep this from happening? What if I had called my father Tuesday and asked him to have dinner with me that night, instead of going out with Sasi? What if I had needed him to help me with something, with anything? What if I had done any of 100 things that could have kept him out of the Sheffield Club that night? Why hadn't I done any of them? Even one? My mind ran in circles again, picturing hundreds of scenarios that led to anything other than my father's funeral.

Like all children, I had imagined my father's funeral at other times in my life. But in those scenarios, I was always an elderly man with my own children and grandchildren supporting me in my grief. And my father? He was ancient, a man who had lived a long full life with my mother, his grandchildren, and great-grandchildren. I never imagined I would be 24 years old. Never.

I worried about my mother and how she would make it through the service. I worried about how I would support her when I wasn't sure I could stand on my own two feet. I worried about my whole family. everyone except my grandma Tzipora, my father's mother, because she would not be there. My father's father had passed away by that time, and my grandmother lived alone. Uncle Moshe had forbidden us to tell her about the murder.

"She's an 87-year-old woman and she lives alone," he pleaded with us. "If you tell her that her Rami was murdered — the son who babied her, who visited her every single day without fail — you'll kill her! I'm telling you she'll have a heart attack or a stroke! We have to protect her."

None of us agreed with him. It was a terrible idea. But he was so adamant and so worried about her physical health, and the rest of us were probably just too exhausted to fight. So we went along. My grandmother would not be at her son's funeral.

The morning of the funeral, I saw my mother already up in the kitchen and went over to rest my head on her shoulder.

"*Ima*, what are we going to do now without *Abba*?" I asked her. "What are we going to do?" It was the rhetorical question winding itself around and around in my mind, and I didn't expect her to answer. But it was the question I knew was on both of our hearts. My mother put her arms around me and we stood together in the kitchen in silence. Just then, one of my aunts walked in to pour some more coffee. She stared at me leaning on my mother.

"Why are you feeling so bad for yourself, Jacob?" she asked. "You're not the one who was murdered. It was your father."

I slowly pushed away from my mother and just stared at my aunt. How could anyone — much less a family member — say such a cruel and heartless thing to someone mourning a parent? At that point, I was in so much pain that I almost wished it *had* been me who had been murdered. But I would never have said that in front of my mother. So I walked out of the room without a comment, just feeling so confused. The only thing I could imagine that would have made my relative say something like that was the intensity of her own pain. This was not an easy journey for any of us.

While I worried about how we would make it through the day and while I mentally kicked and screamed and grabbed for the past, the seconds and minutes moved forward, uncaring. And the time came.

The first thing I noticed is that the house started to empty out. I went to the balcony, and when I looked down to the street, I saw a huge crowd of people. There were so many cars that it was almost impossible for anyone to move. I couldn't watch it, and I went back into the apartment.

Then my Aunt Shoshana came to my mother, Pazit,

Moshe and me carrying some pills and water.

"I think you should all take this before we leave the house," she said. "It will help you relax. It will help you make it through."

I said no.

"Jacob, this will help you," she said, as she took my hand. "It will help your mind to stay clear, so you can understand what is happening around you and you won't be in shock." In the end, I took the pill.

My mother and Pazit left first. I knew it was time when my brother Moshe, Aunt Shoshana, and I were the only ones in the house. We locked the apartment door behind us and took the elevator down. I remember being in that elevator, wondering what could possibly be next. Everything was happening so fast. An entire experience, an entire reality that I had never known before, now happening all around me so quickly.

When the doors opened and I stepped outside, I discovered someone had sent two ambulances to take us to the funeral. Within minutes, one of Aunt Shoshana's daughters fainted and the paramedics ran forward to care for her. Everyone around me was crying, and I wanted to cry so badly, I thought I would explode. But I held in my tears and told myself to be strong, strong. One of my friends asked if I wanted to ride with him to the cemetery, but I thanked him and said no. I needed to be with my mother. I saw her in one of the ambulances, and I climbed in beside her. My mother, Pazit, one cousin, and I rode together. The paramedics closed the doors and started toward the cemetery. It was a slow drive, very slow.

When we arrived at the cemetery, hundreds of people were already filling the streets. I was in such shock, I couldn't walk by myself. Three of my closest friends walked next to me, holding me up. I am not sure where my mother, Pazit, or Moshe were. I assumed they also were walking toward the cemetery with friends and family members. We walked slowly into the cemetery and stopped at a big yard that was already filled with people. I saw a rabbi standing up in front of the crowd.

The funeral began with the traditional ceremony known as *kriah*, in which the rabbi uses a knife to make a cut and then a rip in the black shirts of immediate family members. This identifies us physically as mourners in the community, as do the beards the men grow for 30 days. I did not imagine I could feel any more raw than I already did. But the sound of that fabric ripping again and again in the *kriah* ceremony sounded like my world ripping apart, my heart ripping in two. It was as if we had been marked with a sign of pain, a sign of loss, a physical sign that my father was no longer with us. I wanted to wear that shirt forever — for people to remember Rami Kimchy every time they looked at us.

The men at the funeral all wore black yarmulkes, the skullcaps that show respect to God. My father had purchased some of those yarmulkes the previous week. He came home at the end of a day and handed my mother a package of 25 black yarmulkes.

"What's this?" my mother asked him. "Why would we need so many black yarmulkes?"

"I don't know," he said. "You just never know when you'll need them."

My mother had put them away in a drawer and forgotten about them. Now, they were being worn at his funeral.

The rabbi spoke in front of the crowd, but I couldn't hear what he said above the sounds of so many people crying. Then Dani Nave, the minister of health and a good friend of my Aunt Shoshana, spoke about the situation in Israel and about my family. I could hardly hear his words, either. While he was speaking, one of my cousins came to get me.

"Jacob, you need to come with me," he said. "The rabbis need to get ready to bury the body."

I knew there was no body to bury, but I followed him without saying anything. Pushing through the crowd, I walked with him up to the doorway of small room. Inside were my cousins, my brother Moshe, two of my uncles, and two rabbis. The only male family member missing was my Uncle Nissim, my father's younger brother. A body — a body with two legs — had been laid on a bed in the center of the room, covered by a white shroud, with the head toward the far side from where I was standing.

I immediately recognized this scene — it was exactly as it had been in my dream.

I knew my Uncle Nissim would enter from my left side, exactly as he did a moment later. He stood next to the head of the body and started to cry. And then he took the body in his arms and held it close to him, crying loudly.

I asked one of the rabbis to please come outside with me for a minute. I could barely breathe.

"Jacob, are you all right? Do you need to sit down?" he asked.

With my voice shaking, I told him about my dream five days before the murder. "I saw every single thing. I saw this room, the bed, the body with the white blanket. I saw my Uncle Nissim and the way he hugged my father. I can't believe this. I don't understand."

He had such a kind look on his face.

"Rabbi, is it possible for us to really see the future through our dreams?"

"Yes," he answered. "It is possible. Some of us can. Sometimes it can feel scary, and it's hard for us to understand. But some of us certainly have the ability to see the future in our dreams."

"But if that's true, I could have saved my father. What if I had just spoken with him about the dream, shared the dream? I could have protected him," I said. I felt absolutely destroyed.

"No, no, Jacob," he said. "That's not the way to think about it. What is meant to be is meant to be. You could not have done anything to stop it."

We stayed together for a moment and then went back to the room. Just as we came to the doorway, I saw my Uncle Joseph open the shroud to look at the body. He collapsed, sobbing.

"No one is to touch this," he cried to us. "No one is to open the shroud to look. And no one is to ever ask me what I saw. Ever."

When my Uncle Joseph pulled back the shroud to hold his brother for one last time, I'm sure he had steeled himself to see a mangled and bloodied body. But he was not prepared to see a featureless human form made of plastic. No wonder my poor uncle collapsed in shock. Only my brother, my Uncle Moshe, and I and understood what had happened; we were the only ones who knew that the bombing had left us without a body to bury. Everyone else assumed Uncle Joseph had been overcome by grief and shock, as would anyone who had lost a precious brother. But those of us who had been together at Abu Kabir knew more.

A few people carried the body toward the grave, with hundreds of us walking together. I looked around me to see who had come to share this moment, the last moment for my father. I checked to see if my mother was all right; Pazit and Moshe, too. I looked at the graves around us knowing I would soon start visiting the grave of my father. My sadness, pain, and confusion weighed me down to the ground. I saw ahead of me only endless days filled with this unbearable pain.

We stopped walking and the ceremony started, with everyone wanting to get as close as they could to the grave. I didn't want to look at that hole in the ground. Instead, I looked up to the sky. I asked my father's soul to be with us. I asked God to protect my father, to send him to heaven, to let him rest in peace. I asked God to give him his leg back, to let his arms work perfectly again, and to allow my father to always see us from above, to stay next to us forever.

Each person stepped forward to help shovel dirt to cover the body, as is Jewish tradition. But there was no body to cover.

Why did we have to suffer this extra burden, to not be able to *bury* our loved one, at the very least? Because my father's murderer had chosen to shatter him into the tiniest of pieces, sending bits of his body all over that room, onto the survivors, through the window, and down into the street below. Although I hadn't known it at the time, particles of my father were in the sea of blood I had walked through that night. It's even possible that my shoes carried blood from his body down the stairs and into the street. We come into this world and we leave this world. That's simply a fact of life, and I accept it. But to have nothing left to bury? To have the physical body just disappear in an act of such violence that your brain has no way to make sense of it? No one should have to die like that.

And no one should ever have to stand at a graveside and go through the motions of respectfully burying a shroud covering . . . covering what? I knew the human form supplied by the funeral home was some type of plastic. But to this day, I have obeyed Uncle Joseph's wish: I have never asked him what he saw or what he touched inside that shroud. And as far as I know, neither has any other member of my family.

So this is what Hamas did to us. They ripped our hearts out and forced us to bury a piece of plastic.

I was the last one at the grave, the last one to shovel the dirt. As I did, I heard myself screaming, "Kimchy! Kimchy!" It was the only word I could say. I tried so hard not to cry, but the tears came out and I just couldn't stop them. When I put the shovel down, my friends came up to hold me. We grabbed onto each other so tightly, feeling the loss in every inch of our bodies.

I drove back to the apartment with my friends. I sat in the car and tried to picture what came next. Why was time still moving forward?

. . .

The house was filled with people immediately after the funeral and every day for a month. Shiva usually lasts a week, and is even shortened by certain holidays, which was the case following my father's murder. But really, it hardly mattered that the formal shiva ended so soon. Our home was constantly crowded with people.

They would start arriving early in the morning — family, neighbors, people we grew up with, friends from the army and college, my brothers' and sisters' friends and, of course, friends of my parents. Occasionally, we had a visit from a member of parliament or a government minister. Every now and then, the news media would come to the door, and we would send one of my uncles outside to speak with them.

Some friends who had lost their parents tried to tell me what the coming days and months might be like. I appreciated their love and concern, and I listened to everything they had to say, to any advice they could give me. But always in my mind was the thought that they really didn't *know* because they had no idea what I had experienced at the site of that attack.

I had said nothing to anyone about it — what I was still seeing in front of my eyes all the time, the stench that would come up in my nostrils, the blaring and chaotic noise screaming in my ears. I could not make the words come out of my mouth. And why would I? So other people could suffer the torment I had in my head? No. Those memories did not need to be shared. I kept my friends close and appreciated their love and concern and their commitment to just *be* with me.

There were moments, of course, when I would have liked a little privacy from the crowds — when I would open the door to my room and find friends using my computer to take care of their business, or when someone would tell a joke and the sound of laughter would make me feel out of place in my own home. What was going on here? Was this a party? Where was my father? At times like that, I would go sit next to my mother and just rest my head on her shoulder, sometimes closing my eyes to try to find a moment's peace.

I definitely wanted and needed everyone to be there for us, and appreciated them all! But sometimes I just needed quiet. I didn't know at the time that all mourners feel that way, wanting one thing and then the next as your mind and body try to adjust to your suddenly new reality.

Having the house filled with people was a godsend for my mother. So many people came to show how much they loved us and to show her that she wasn't alone. People brought food, coffee, tea, whatever we needed for ourselves and our guests. They took care of the house, washed the dishes and the floors, and sometimes didn't leave until after midnight, until the house was spotless and my mother had been put to bed.

What would we have done without them?

The house was so crowded that I really didn't have much time alone with Moshe or Pazit. But one afternoon just a few days after the funeral, Moshe called me into his room and closed his door. He had a wide-eyed frightened look on his face.

"Jacob, I don't know what I'm going to do," he said to me.

"What do you mean?"

"I always knew I couldn't fall down because *Abba* was standing right behind us to help us up, to hold us up. But now, I don't know what I'm going to do. I feel like I could come crashing down at any moment."

It was so very hard for me to see Moshe like this. He was the older brother who had never been the least bit emotional or demonstrative. I didn't know how to help. So I sat down on his bed and told him the same thing I kept telling myself.

"We're going to be OK. You and me and Pazit, we have each other. And we have *Ima* to take care of. We're going to be OK, Moshe. Everything will be OK."

But he just looked at me with a blank face. Did he believe what I said to him? I hope so. It was all the comfort I had to offer at the time.

Did I believe it? No. Not for a minute. I was absolutely lost.

I would be talking to a friend or relative at the house, feeling almost calm for a moment, and suddenly scenes from the bombing site would appear in my vision. I would see again the man impaled on the club's front window, half his body hanging over the street. I would smell the room filled with blood and see the decapitated head in the corner. The police sirens would scream at me.

The person I'd been speaking with would want to know

how to help, what time to put dinner on the table, or when my mother should lie down for a rest. But my mind had carried me far from that conversation straight into hell. My heart would start racing and my face would begin to sweat. I would have to excuse myself. What was happening to me?

After the first week, I allowed myself to get away from the house at times when I couldn't face answering phones or making decisions. Some days, I would go to the beach to just sit and listen to the waves, so steady and constant. I would try to think, try to process everything that had happened to me. But I didn't know how. The same thoughts and images would come at me over and over. I never could find myself.

I would go to the cemetery several times a week. I had such a strong need to see the sign with my father's name on it, I could hardly get there fast enough. I knew his body wasn't buried there. I knew *he* wasn't there. But still, it was the only place where I felt I could really talk to my father. At the cemetery, I felt he was coming down from heaven to be with me, to listen to me, to hear my words. The cemetery felt holy to me, the place where I believe I will unite with my father again in the future. The only other place I felt that type of closeness to my father was at the site of the bombing, on the street where the Sheffield Club had been — the place where my father's soul had left this earth for heaven.

Alone at the cemetery, I would talk to my father, cry, scream, whatever I needed to do. Once, I went at night and fell asleep on his grave. It felt good. I found a tiny bit of comfort sleeping next to his name, some small respite from the pain, the memories, the terror, and my conviction that I would feel this lost forever.

One afternoon about two weeks after my father's murder, the apartment was filled with people when we heard a loud explosion and the whole building started shaking. Through the windows, we saw all the birds in the neighborhood fly up together at once.

People immediately began screaming. Some people ran out to the balcony. Others called family and friends to see what they knew. The apartment was in chaos.

Everyone was upset, frightened, panicked. But no one was more affected than Moshe. He ran out to the balcony, and I could see the tears running down his face as he screamed from his fear and his pain — the fear that we would lose another family member, another friend, someone else we knew. It hurt so badly to see my brother in so much pain.

Some of his friends ran to help him, to comfort and hug him. They brought him indoors, and we turned on the television to wait for the news.

We learned this explosion was a young man in the process of blowing himself to bits in a park just a quarter-mile from my mother's apartment — a park where old people would sit and play cards. Two people were murdered that day. We didn't know them, but we cried anyway. We cried for their pain, for our pain, for a life that seemed filled with more fear and pain than anyone could tolerate. We watched the news report until we heard the words "Abu Kabir." Then we turned the TV off.

Thirty days after my father's murder, we gathered at his grave again, following tradition. It was also time for the men to have their beards cut as a sign that the period of mourning was over. Local barbers would remove the beards at no charge out of respect. I didn't want to participate, though. I wanted to keep this physical sign of loss on me, an outward sign of my pain at losing my father. But I went along and had my beard removed because I knew I was expected to. And suddenly, there I was in the mirror with my clean face.

Who was I without these physical signs of mourning?

Now that my beard was gone, would people think everything was OK? That my pain was over? That my family is OK and back to normal?

Everything was definitely not OK. And I had no idea how to handle the excruciating pain that wrapped itself around me every minute.

I decided to talk to my supervisor at the video store because I knew he had suffered a loss, too. He agreed to meet me. We talked for a few minutes about the store, about the town, and he gave me his condolences again. Then I began to ask the question I had come for.

"I know you lost your brother, and I can't tell you how sorry I am about that. This isn't easy, but I need to know something."

"OK. What's that?"

"I want to know how long it will take before I feel fine again."

The manager looked closely at my face. "What do you mean by 'feel fine again?'"

"When will I feel normal?"

He took a deep breath. "Jacob, no one can answer that question for you. I'm sorry," he said slowly. His voice was soft. "But time will eventually heal your feelings. You have to give yourself a lot of time. Don't rush anywhere."

That was not what I had wanted to hear. I wanted to *know*. How much pain would I have to bear? Would I have to wait three months? Four months? A year? Or would I break under the agony that almost took away my breath every single day?

Looking back, I can hardly imagine what my supervisor must have thought about a question that was both so personal and so naive. I'd clearly had no previous experience with death and mourning. But he responded with kindness, and I appreciated that.

Others were not so kind. At the time of my father's murder, I was dating a girl who lived out of the country. We spoke every day and before long, she came to visit. She was caring, compassionate, and wonderful to me and to my family in every way. But when I saw her father, he had a different view.

"Come take a ride with me, Jacob," he said to me one day. "I'd like a chance to talk to you." An Israeli himself, I assumed he would understand our lives and be sympathetic to our loss at the hands of Hamas. I was wrong.

"Jacob, I know my daughter likes you very much, and I know you care for her, too. But no one likes to be around a person who's sad all the time. If you want to keep dating my daughter, you really need to put a smile on your face. I want her to be happy," he said to me in the car. "You need to think about that."

His words, his complete lack of empathy, hit me with almost a physical force. I sat with him in silence. What could I say to this man? I knew his daughter didn't share those feelings. But with a father like that, I also knew our relationship could not be permanent — and it wasn't.

Eventually, the constant crowds at home began to lessen. On the one hand, I was glad to have some privacy back. The apartment began to feel a bit more normal when I was there with just Moshe and our mother. On the other, I was terrified of being alone and facing the reality of restarting my life. The three of us needed some privacy, but we didn't want to be alone.

It was at around this time that my grandma Tzipora found out about her son's death. Before the funeral, my Uncle Moshe called her to say that Rami had to make a sudden trip to the States to take care of his prosthetic leg. The next week it was another excuse, and then another. But not too many weeks later, the truth came out when a cleaning lady in my grandma's building said how sorry she was about her loss.

My poor grandma was crushed -- not only beneath the weight of her son's death, but beneath the deceit that kept her from mourning with the support of family and friends. It was every mother's most terrifying nightmare made unnecessarily worse, even if from good intentions. The rest of us offered what comfort we could. We hugged her, we kissed her, we cried together and held her close. But it wasn't enough.

My grandma wanted to go through the entire shiva again, including the *kriah* ceremony. She wanted the outward signs of our tradition to identify her as a mourner, so people would know of Rami Kimchy. She felt exactly as we had, so we understood.

My Aunt Shoshana called a rabbi, explained our story, and asked him to come do the *kriah* ceremony for my grandma. But he refused. The *kriah* ceremony is to be done at the time of the funeral, and that was something my grandmother had missed.

We did the next best thing for her. We told her she could come every day to our home as if it were the original shiva. We would be here for her, we would sit with her, cry with her, talk about my father. And when she wasn't at our home, we made sure family members were with her so she wouldn't be alone at her home.

As time went on, my friends continued to try to help as best as they could. Although I felt so removed from them and from their lives that had continued on just as before, I knew they genuinely cared about me. One friend gave me a gift certificate for a massage, something I had never experienced, and I thought I might as well give it a try. I was surprised to find I absolutely loved it. For the first time since my father's death, I felt truly relaxed. On the way home from the massage, my phone rang. I decided I would recommend a massage to whomever was calling me.

But it was a friend who worked at the town's emergency center and she was screaming.

"Jacob! Where are you? Where are you right now?" I started to sweat.

When I told her where I was, not too far from my home, she yelled again. "Stop! Stop your car! Turn around and go in the other direction! "

"Why? I have to get home. What's happening?"

But there was no need to ask. I felt the familiar panic rising, my stomach churning. I knew what was happening.

"There's a terrorist, a scene up ahead. He has a bomb in his car."

"I have to get to my mother!"

"No! Turn around!"

That's when I saw police with machine guns all around me. I turned the car back and took another way home, driving as fast as I could. I didn't care what my friend said. If a terrorist were nearby, I would not let my mother face this alone. I sped through the streets.

The police were successful this time. The terrorist was apprehended very close to our apartment. No one died — *this* time.

. . .

As the weeks went on, things settled down a bit, and we were able to again take care of the small tasks that make a household run — paperwork, insurance, bills, a little cooking, etc. On some days, we might even have looked like normal people walking through the house, eating together, watching TV, playing with my niece and nephew when Pazit came by for a visit. But nothing was normal.

I felt suddenly aware of how many people in this world are angry or disappointed for reasons that were no longer of any importance to me. Whatever the problem, chances are it could be fixed. But when you lose someone you love, when he is dead and gone, there is *nothing* you can do to change the situation. You can scream and scream for the rest of your life. You can sleep on the person's grave cradling a piece of his clothing in your arms. You can give every penny you own to the poor. You can read every philosophy book ever written, talk to every rabbi, priest, minister.

But nothing, nothing will ever bring the person back.

Not knowing what else to do to cope with my feelings, I started taking my car out for a drive at night. I would drive it faster and faster until I took it up to 120 miles per hour. With the music blaring as loud as it could go, I would listen to the same song over and over, "Brothers in Arms" by the band Dire Straits with the words "every man has to die." And every time I got to that line, thinking about my father, I would cry and scream at the top of my lungs. I would drive faster and faster, trying with all my energy to scream all the pain out of my body, just wanting to crash my car into a wall. I would drive on and on every night until eventually I would ease up on the gas, my emotions spent but never healed.

I would slow down, drive home, kiss my mother, and go to my room, where I would do everything I possibly could to stay awake. Because it was around this time that the nightmares began.

In my initial nightmares, I would be looking for my father. The location would change, but the basic story was always the same. My family and friends would be with me at a restaurant, playing soccer, going to the beach, or into the woods. We would be looking for my father until a man ran up screaming, "God is great!" And then we would all die.

In another, I would be at my wedding with my father and the whole family. I would be standing under the wedding canopy with my beautiful bride and the rabbi — the happiest moment of my life. Then a man would run up and blow himself to pieces, and we would all die.

In some dreams, I would try to run, only to discover I had lost my legs and hands. In others, I would see my father at a party inside a nearby building. I would run in and grab him. But when he turned toward me, it wasn't him, and I would run out of the building screaming and crying. Where was my father?

In still another dream, my father had disappeared, and all my friends had gathered to help me look for him. We looked everywhere and finally found him in the ocean. But when I lifted my father up in my arms, I saw that his body had been ripped to shreds. It was as if someone had cut him with a knife, cutting and cutting over and over.

I sometimes woke up from these nightmares screaming with such force that I felt the building would shake. Even with my door closed and my mother's door closed, my cries were so loud they would wake her, and she would come running to comfort me with sugar and water.

Those nightmares were a bomb of sadness going off in my gut. They took me straight back to the Sheffield Club, to the moment I saw my father's taxi, to the pain that wrestled my soul to the ground. It would sometimes take days for me to put those dreams behind me, to feel released from that exhausting, extra layer of pain.

And yet, not all my dreams were nightmares.

In one particular dream, my father would come to the apartment, and I would be so happy to see him.

I would run up to him and just hold him so tight, burying my face in his neck, taking in his scent, feeling his arms around me, too.

"*Abba! Abba*, where have you been?" I would ask every time as I drew back to look at his face, my hands still on his shoulders.

He would never answer that question with words. But every time, he would look straight in my eyes with his wonderful smile, always smiling. I was so thrilled to be with him that I felt my heart would burst with happiness — the same happiness I felt as a child when I jumped into his arms.

In the first few minutes of waking from a dream like that, I could never be sure if my father were alive or dead. I wouldn't know where I was or what I was feeling. But one thing I was always sure about: It had been so wonderful to hold my father in my arms, even in a dream.

As I tried to stay awake at night, I would think about everything that had happened and try to make some sense of it all. I never really succeeded. But I noticed that one question came up over and over: Where was God in all of this?

As a child, when my father's accident left him near death and then in pain for so many years, I gave up any belief in God I might have had at the time. The God I believed in simply wouldn't have let something so horrible happen to such a good person. Consequently, I reasoned, God did not exist. It never occurred to me through the intervening years that God might very well exist, just not in the very simplistic framework I had imaged as a child.

But now, after the very worst thing imaginable had happened to my father, I found myself starting to believe in God again. Why had such a hideous tragedy taken the life of such a wonderful person? I did not know — and I realized I would never know. But as an adult, I found myself willing to put that question to the side and still consider the possibility of God's existence.

In fact, I suddenly felt I *had* to believe in God. I *had*

to believe in something greater than myself. Why? Because I had two experiences around the time of my father's death that could not be attributed to any other source.

First, because there was absolutely no other way to explain my dream of my father's funeral. Five days before his death, all was right with the world and I had no hint of what was to come. Then I lay down to sleep and a dream showed me exactly what my father's funeral would look like later that week. Where did that come from? How did it happen?

And second, because my father visited me on the third night of the shiva.

I woke up at about 3 o'clock that morning to hear my father's voice next to me in my room. I knew I needed to open my eyes to see what was happening, but I was afraid. So with my eyes still closed, I reached out to touch the wall that should be next to me. It was there. Next I pinched myself to make sure I was awake. I was.

I opened my eyes and saw a big circle of white light, brightest in the middle and faded a bit toward the edges. The light moved very slowly toward the window, eventually leaving the room.

I got out of bed immediately and went into the kitchen to make some strong coffee. I wanted to stay awake, to make sure I would remember the song and the light and wouldn't think it was a dream.

About an hour later, my mother came into the kitchen.

"What are you doing up so early?" she asked me.

"*Ima,* I have to tell you something that's going to sound very strange. But it's completely true: *Abba* visited me this morning."

I told her everything that had happened, every detail I could remember. She was shocked, and she found it hard to believe, which I certainly understood. If the experience happened to someone else, I would have thought they sounded crazy. But what I told her was the absolute truth, and I promised myself to cherish that memory in my heart for the rest of my life.

I did not have all the answers. But I knew with certainty there is something more to this world than what we touch and feel in our everyday lives. I was starting to believe that the "something" was God.

CHAPTER NINE

A Ray of Light

Eventually, our friends and relatives went back to the lives they had left. My own friends went back to the army, to work, to school, to their families. Pazit went back to her house, focusing her attention on her husband and children. But my mother, Moshe, and I were just lost in the apartment that now seemed so big and so empty. Where was everyone? Where was my father?

The three of us watched TV from time to time, mostly the news. We talked about the state of affairs in Israel and wondered how we could possibly continue to live with terrorism infecting our daily lives, such a vicious disease. We talked about my father quite a lot—about what to do with his belongings, his papers, how much we missed him.

We talked about what we had learned after his death — that my father didn't always charge his clients. He might write down what fare he was owed, but he never went back to collect it. We talked about the fact that it was never about the money to him; it was always about the people and the fact that he was so happy to be out working and interacting in the community again.

We talked and talked. But we managed to avoid the single biggest issue that terrified each of us: Now what?

Now what? What would life look like without my father? We had absolutely no idea.

I felt exactly what Moshe had expressed to me during the shiva: My father had always been my rock, my foundation. Without his support, his wisdom, his strong arms around me, what was holding me up? The answer was that nothing was holding me up, nothing was holding all of us up. And I was terrified. It felt as if I had stepped into a new and completely unfamiliar country — not understanding the language, not knowing anyone, filled with all questions and no answers. There was no respite from the pain. Not during the day. Not at night.

And yet, I never spoke to Moshe about this. Other than the one shiva afternoon in his bedroom, he never spoke to me about it, either. It might have helped us to talk about these terrifying feelings we shared. It might have helped Moshe to know he wasn't alone in his fears. It could have been comforting for each of us to have had *one* person with whom we could be honest and acknowledge the true depth of our pain. But it never happened.

Moshe eventually went back to work and tried to seem as normal as possible, putting on a brave face and pushing himself forward. I put my brave face on, too. I wanted to be strong, and I believed it was expected of me as the best way to support my brother and mother. The three of us all worked so hard to keep our pain inside. It was absolutely exhausting.

My friends did everything they could to support me. They called, they texted, they emailed, they came by to keep me company. Many of my friends had genuinely loved my father, too, and were grieving his murder as a very deep and personal loss. It comforted me to know how important my father had been in their lives, to know they would never, ever forget Rami Kimchy. And it comforted me to share their sadness.

But my friends also wanted to get on with things, and I understood that, too.

One night, they planned for some of us to go to a bar in Tel Aviv. I had decided I would really try to have a good time, and the evening started out great. But before we even got into the bar, we suddenly heard a very loud noise. We didn't know what it was — maybe a car backfiring or a large truck slamming a door — but we knew it was *not* a gun or a bomb.

Nevertheless, my body reacted instantaneously as if the noise were another attack. I tried to calm myself; I *knew* I was not in danger. But my heart was jumping wildly in my chest, my hands were sweating, and I felt the nausea rising inside me. I didn't want to let them down, but I told my friends I had to leave. I had to get home. I just couldn't do it.

. . .

My father's murder occurred at the beginning of May, just before the final exams of my sophomore year. I didn't really care about college or anything else at that point, but I had promised my father I would graduate, so I knew I had to finish the semester. I had no idea how I would do it, but I had no choice. By the time I went back to the school to meet with the dean, I had already missed several exams.

"Of course, we'll support you in any way we can," he told me. "You take your exams whenever you feel ready. And if you need to take them again, you can do that, too. You can take them each several times if you need to."

"Thank you. I appreciate that. I really do," I said. "But I just don't know how to prepare for them. I can't focus on anything. I don't know what to do about it."

"Why don't we put together a study group to help you? Please, Jacob, let us do that much for you. I know your classmates want to help."

I appreciated his offer and his kindness, and I certainly didn't have any better plan. So I agreed to meet with the students.

The study group was awkward for me from the beginning. Weeks earlier, we had all been sophomores together, friends and cohorts urging each other forward together as a team. But now, they had taken their exams and were starting their junior year. I, on the other hand, was a sophomore who seemed to have forgotten everything I'd learned. Each time we met, I felt confused and out of place. What was I doing? Why did this matter to me? I had no energy for it.

More than once during the study group, the scene at the Sheffield Club would suddenly appear in front of my eyes. I could hear the talk about economics or finance continuing around me, but I sensed I was no longer in the room. Instead, I would feel the sticky slime of blood under my feet. I would see limbs piled up in front of me. As my stomach turned over and I started to sweat, I would have to excuse myself to go home — from a study session that was being held solely for my benefit.

I felt so guilty that these students were giving so much and getting nothing from me in return. I wasn't the least bit engaged with them, and I'm sure they knew it. After three sessions, I just couldn't go on with it. Since I didn't know what else to do, I decided to just take the exams and see what happened. The dean approved.

I decided to take the finance exam first. The dean set me up in a room alone with the exam and told me my time limit. Less than 10 minutes later, I left the room. I don't remember if I even wrote my name on the paper. I just could not do it.

I decided to try once more, this time with accounting. But the same thing happened, and again, I ran from the room.

What was happening to me? I seemed to have completely lost control over my body and my emotions — and that in itself added to my fear. I couldn't calm myself. I couldn't keep my heart from racing or repress the feeling that I would vomit. I just could not think straight — about anything.

I went back to my dean. I thanked him for his efforts on my behalf and told him I couldn't do it. He said he understood and realized that I just wasn't ready. He said he would allow me to take the sophomore exams again the following May and encouraged me to come back. I thanked him and left.

At home, I talked it over with my mother.

"I know I'll have to wait an entire year to become a junior. But I don't know what else to do. I just can't do it. I don't have any other options," I told her. But she saw it differently.

"No. You absolutely can't lose this entire year, Jacob. You need to take the exams now, while the school is still giving you that opportunity. You have to take them again."

"But, *Ima*, I can't!" I told her. "I tried. I can't think straight. When I look at the book, I don't know what I'm reading. It's just words floating on the page to me. The charts and graphs are just drawings that mean nothing to me. Nothing makes sense."

"Jacob, I understand that it's hard for you to concentrate now. I really do." She spoke in a soft voice and reached around to gently rub my back. "It's hard for all of us to think straight right now. But I know that going to school is the right thing for you."

"I'll do it next year. You know I made a promise to *Abba*, and you know I'll keep that promise. No matter what, I will graduate."

"I really think this year is better for you."

I did not know what to do, so I turned to my friends, exhausted and feeling absolutely defeated. I had always been the problem solver in our group of friends. Everyone turned to me for support. If they couldn't find a job or a parent was unemployed, I told them not to worry. With complete confidence, I said they would find a new job. I spoke with them about options, ideas and possibilities. If they had broken up with a girlfriend — or worse, she had broken up with them — I told them that within a few months, they would be with someone new in a better relationship.

I spent time with them, we went out together, I introduced them to new dates and always discussed ways to find a new partner. I didn't just say these things, I believed them. Because if my father could come back from his accident to be the strong man that all my friends knew and loved, then truly anything was possible!

But now it was my turn. I had a problem with no solution — an attitude they had never, ever heard from me — and I needed their help. While I was sharing my problem and the questions I had for myself about college, one of my friends asked if I had heard about the school from the U.K. that had just opened a few campuses in Israel, one of which was in our town. It was called the University of Derby. Maybe, they suggested, it would have a different schedule. I looked into it and discovered that was the case. The university would accept the transfer credits from my current school, and I could begin in October, instead of having to wait the full year.

I enrolled, so grateful that my friends had helped me find a solution to satisfy both my mother and myself. I knew I had a few months before school started, instead of having to rush to class at that moment. The new schedule allowed me to relax a bit.

. . .

A few months after my father's death and before classes started at the new college, I asked my mother a question that had been nagging at me every day.

"*Ima*, when there's a terrorist attack, what do you think happens to all the personal things that are left behind?"

"We got what we could from your father's taxi, Jacob. You know that. We'll always have those things to keep."

"I know. But what if there's more? What if there are items, things that someone collected at the scene?"

"Who would collect such things?"

"I don't know. Do you think the police collected anything?"

"The police? Why would they bother? It's not like they have to collect evidence."

"I know. But how would you feel if I went to the police station to ask? Would you be all right with that?"

"If that's what you want," she said. "If you're sure you want to go there, Jacob, it's OK with me."

I just couldn't stop wondering if something of my father's might still be out there. If it were, I wanted it. I needed it, to hold it in my hands. Maybe it would tell me something about what happened that night.

So I went to the police station in Rishon Lezion. I walked up to the desk and spoke to the first police officer I saw.

"I have a bit of a weird question," I started. The officer stared at me. "What's the chance that you collected personal items from the Sheffield Club attack?"

He asked me to wait there. A few minutes later another man walked up and introduced himself as the station psychologist.

"You're asking about the personal effects we collected from the attack in May?"

I introduced myself and explained why I was interested. "Do you have anything I can see?"

"Actually, we do have artifacts from the attack," he said.

"That's good. Can I see them?"

He hesitated. "Are you sure you want to do that?"

"Yes, I'm sure. There could be something of my father's in there."

"You're free to look through them if you'd like. But you might want to take a minute to think about it. It wouldn't be easy."

"I understand," I told him. "But can I please see what you have? Now?"

The psychologist took me into the station's basement and sat me down at a table. He brought over two large, heavy black bags.

"This is everything we have," he said. He looked at me, started to say something and stopped. And then he said, "I'll be upstairs if you need me."

I felt like I was in a horror movie — in the dark basement of a police station looking for clues to a hideous mass murder, which was exactly what I was doing. When I opened the bags, I found myself sifting through dozens and dozens of wallets, broken cell phones, eyeglass frames, and car keys — each covered in layers of dried blood and dirt. My hands moved slowly through the pieces, knowing that each item was precious; each one telling the story of a life that meant everything to someone else. There was a belt buckle, a metal watchband with no face. And then I saw my father's keys.

My father's keys. I suddenly felt as if I had won the lottery. I was ecstatic to have found something that had belonged to him, something that connected me to him. But even though I would have recognized them anywhere, the sight of them left me in shock.

His key ring was a thick metal circle, the type with a slit you can just barely open to slide on another ring or a very thin key, moving it around and around the layers of the metal circle until it pops into place. There was the mangled key to his Mercedes taxi and another mangled key to our apartment. But what took my breath away was the key ring itself. This heavy metal ring had been bent in on itself and twisted around so that it almost formed two circles now instead of the original one. These keys had been in my father's pocket or in his hand when the bomb exploded. If an explosion could twist such a strong piece of metal, what did it do to my father? I couldn't stop those painful thoughts.

I doubt my mother was expecting me to bring anything home from the police station that day. I, too, hadn't really thought I would have any success. When I walked into the house and handed her my father's keys, she gasped. We hugged each other but didn't say anything. There was no need.

. . .

Just before I was to start my new college, a girl I was dating asked me to join her and her parents on a trip to the Bahamas. A cruise? Me? I told her I couldn't possibly go.

"I really appreciate it and I'd love to spend the time with you," I told her. "But my father *just* died. I can't go on a trip and pretend to have a good time. And I can't leave my *ima.*"

"Your father died over three months ago, Jacob. It didn't just happen. You have to think about moving forward with your life," she said.

"But to me, it did just happen."

My mother agreed with her.

"Jacob, this is an opportunity for you to get out and

have a good time. They are so nice to include you, and I absolutely think you should go," she said. "I think you *need* to go. Moshe will be here with me. You have nothing to worry about."

Everyone told me I should go, and so I changed my mind and went. They all thought I would have been thrilled. After all, here I was on a ship, under the stars with my girlfriend and her family. But grief isn't an article of clothing you choose when to wear and when to leave behind, and the truth is I was miserable. At home I could at least be myself, whatever that new self was. But here with this family — people who were kind enough to share their vacation with me but who couldn't understand what we had just been through — I used all my energy to act normal at meals and activities, pretending I was all right and truly enjoying their generosity. In reality, I was counting the days until I could see my mother again, and just be in the house with her and Moshe. No matter what anyone said, I felt so guilty for leaving them.

One night, we all attended a show together on the ship. But this time, I just couldn't sit through it. I apologized and said I would wait for them outside the theater, sitting down next to the double glass doors so I could see them when they came out. I looked at the beautiful blue water and the deep blue sky. I missed my father so much, and I started speaking to him in my mind. I had heard — and I wanted to believe — that the souls of the dead stay with the family for a while before turning permanently to heaven.

"*Abba*," I said to him silently, "I want to believe that you are right here with me. If you are with me, can you let me know? Can you give me a sign? Please, *Abba,* any kind of sign so I will know that you and your love are with me. You know how much I love you and how much I miss you."

A few seconds later, the elevator doors opened. Out

walked a man with one crutch. I could tell by his walk that he had a prosthetic leg. The man turned to me directly and smiled, but he said nothing. Then he turned back and walked — with exactly my father's gait — into the hall where the show was in progress.

What had just happened? I was dumbstruck. Had I just asked my father for a sign and had he given me one within seconds? That's what I believed. I felt my father's warm love and his message bathing my heart. It was as clear to me as if he had said, "Jacob, follow this man, follow this example. Go back into the show. Enjoy yourself. Be happy. Continue your life. I'm here and I love you."

I immediately opened the door to the show to look for this man, but I couldn't find him then and I never saw him again. I did find my girlfriend, though. I sat down next to her, held her hand, and leaned over to whisper to her.

"Thank you for saving my seat," I said with a smile. "I want to enjoy the rest of the show with you." And I kissed her lightly on the ear.

When I came home from the trip, I shared that story with my mother. Just like the night my father visited me during the shiva, my mother didn't really know what to say or how to react. I didn't blame her. But this time, she had an experience of her own to tell me.

It seems that when Pazit and the children came over one evening, the baby broke my mother's brand new glasses. Pazit and my mother both tried to fix them, but couldn't. Pazit was upset and apologetic, but my mother told her not to worry.

"I'll take them to the store in the morning and get them fixed."

When she came down to breakfast the next morning, though, the glasses had been fixed and she put them on to read the paper. She thanked Moshe when he came into the kitchen.

"For what?"

"For fixing my glasses. I thought I'd have to take them to the store."

"Why? I thought your glasses were brand new," he said as he poured some coffee.

"They were new," my mother said. "But the baby broke them last night, and Pazit and I couldn't fix them. Didn't you fix them?"

"No. I didn't know they were broken."

That stopped my mother. "But how did they get fixed if you didn't do it?"

"I have no idea."

She called Pazit just to confirm that she hadn't imagined the baby breaking the glasses.

"Of course you didn't imagine it," Pazit said. "You're taking them to the store this morning, right?" They went round and round for bit. But the facts were the facts: When my mother went to bed, her new glasses were broken; when she woke up, they were fixed. In the meantime, no one had touched them.

Some people faced with this story would assume that at least one person was joking or even lying. Others would be satisfied leaving it with no explanation. But my mother and I believed we knew who fixed the glasses, and that's the story we plan to keep in our hearts. I knew it didn't make "sense." But who was to say he was not taking care of us still?

. . .

When I started back to college that October, I can't honestly say that I cared. Everything I previously had enjoyed about college — the student discussions, the research, intellectual encounters, challenging conversations with professors

— none of it held the least bit of interest for me. I dragged myself through the classes and through the material. But my focus was on processing the loss in my family, and my heart was heavy with questions that could never be answered in a classroom.

When I looked around the room at the other students who seemed so involved in the work, in the banter with the professor, I felt so removed from their lives and their concerns. I would occasionally hear the conversation continue around me but sense that I was no longer in the classroom. I would see the body of the man impaled on the Sheffield Club window or smell the black smoke that poured out around him. I would see again the ocean of blood or visions from my nightmares of the previous night, and I would have to leave the classroom to go outside and cry. At breaks between classes, I would look at my friends smiling, laughing, sharing stories about life. Most of the time, I would walk past them to find a seat in the back row and wait there for the next class to start — just staring at my books, talking to no one. Sometimes I took my bag and just left. I would go to the beach, meet my friends, or get a coffee and take a long walk.

When I'd enrolled at Derby, I hadn't said a word to anyone about what I was going through. The school knew I was transferring from another nearby university, but no one knew why. I didn't tell them. My teachers had no idea what I was living through. Even my new classmates, my new friends, knew nothing. I didn't want them to think I was different or needed special treatment in any way. I wanted to be strong. And besides, I just couldn't talk about it.

But eventually, it became more than I could handle. I knew my mother would be upset, but I had to quit. I just could not do it. I went to speak to the dean first, to explain why I couldn't make it, telling her what I was going through and why I was too distracted to focus on school. She was so kind and supportive, and we spoke for quite a while. She told me she believed in me and believed I could do it. She said the department would support me with any help I needed. She pleaded with me to stay. I couldn't imagine how I would succeed. By this point, I felt that the life was draining out of me and I had no idea how to stop it. But I went back into the classroom to try again.

Slowly I did develop relationships with some of the students and professors, and slowly I felt more comfortable in class. But a deep, intent focus on my studies continued to elude me.

The Israeli government was not oblivious to the fact that so many citizens were emotionally damaged and suffering from the terror that had become part of our daily lives. The state didn't offer much in the way of help — certainly not enough — but it did officially associate itself with one nonprofit organization, the Terror Victims' Association. A few months after my father's murder, my mother had gone to the Association for some information, but found it disorganized and frustrating. When she spoke to someone there about her frustration, the woman said, "Lady, if you want this organization to ever get better, you'll have to get involved. Otherwise it will never happen, and you might as well not complain."

And so my mother began to volunteer at the Association, helping the victims of terrorism who came there for support. At her request, I volunteered with her at the office a few times after class. I would help find a location for an event, fold invitations for a mailing, or make some phone calls. I didn't do much, but those hours I spent at the Terror Victims Association changed my life in a very real way.

My mother and I saw victims of all ages, and we listened to their stories. We saw people who were physically alive, yet so lost that they would likely never find their way back to a full life. We saw people who had lost someone in the First Intifada 10 years earlier and had never since been able to hold a job to support themselves or feed their families. We saw people who couldn't maintain their most cherished relationships — people who broke off an engagement, or who divorced their spouse of 30 years — because the stress of maintaining a life with another human being was more than they could bear. We heard stories of mothers and fathers who became completely disconnected from their living children because they had never recovered from losing a child in a suicide bombing.

All the stories were heartbreaking. But one stood out above the others. Avi had been a successful and happy businessman, married with two children. One day as he sat in his office in Tel Aviv, a suicide bomber blew himself up on a bus just below his office window. As the building shook violently from the blast, blood and bits of human flesh exploded up through the open window, landing on Avi.

Physically, Avi was not injured, and all his loved ones were safe and sound. But he was so traumatized from the shock of being covered in the blood and flesh of the murder victims that he became unable to function and had to be hospitalized. Eventually, he stopped talking and required constant physical assistance. Avi never went back to work, and eventually lost contact with his friends and even family members. The only way he ever communicated again was through the art he created with his hands.

All of these men and women wanted to be the people they had been before such tragedy struck, but they didn't know how to get there. It was terribly painful to hear so many bitter and sad people talk — those who could speak — with such longing about the people they once had been. None of them wanted to be just confused, disabled, hollowed-out shadows of their formers selves.

My short time volunteering at the Association absolutely terrified me, because I recognized the person I could easily become.

Would I end up being nothing but a shadow of the strong, joyful college student I had been when I headed out that night with my friend Sasi? Had Jacob Kimchy disappeared forever along with my father? Where was that Jacob? What was happening to me? I was so frightened and confused.

It was very difficult for my mother and I to talk about the terrorism survivors we saw at the Association, to find the words to discuss the fears we had for ourselves and for each other, to hear those words come out of our mouths. But we did it.

I was so proud of my mother; she could have retreated into silence, and no one would have blamed her if she had. But she did not. My mother had always been a strong woman, but now she became a superhero to me. Together, we forced ourselves to struggle through some very difficult conversations. And together, we vowed we would *not* become like the survivors we had seen.

We knew we needed help. And we knew we wanted to help others.

My mother was the first to begin seeing a social worker. After her first few meetings, the social worker asked to meet with the whole family. Moshe and Pazit said no. They absolutely refused to meet with anyone and made it clear they did not want to be asked again. I, too, said no, at first. But after thinking it through, and even though I was very anxious about it, I agreed to go with my mother. I wasn't comfortable talking with strangers about my feelings or my fears, so I couldn't imagine what the meeting would be like.

When I arrived at the appointment, I was absolutely tense, prepared to protect my emotions from assault. But when the door opened, I saw a very short middle-aged lady with a very big smile.

"Come in! Come in! Sarah, it's so good to see you!" She hugged my mother.

"And you must be Jacob." She took my outstretched hand with both of hers. "I'm Esther. I am so happy to meet you!"

"Glad to meet you, too."

And as soon as I said it, I realized I meant it sincerely. This woman's beautiful spirit was immediately apparent to me, and I couldn't help but smile right back at her as I felt instantly enveloped by her kindness. I still didn't know what the next hour would bring, but I could feel myself relax as she ushered us into her office,.

We spoke about my father that day, about my friends, school, and how I was feeling in general. My mother said she was very worried about my nightmares.

"You know, Jacob, I believe I know a good psychologist who could help you," Esther said. "I believe he could help you get over these feelings and these nightmares."

"That's not what I'm not looking for," I told her.

"Really? Why is that?"

"Because I don't want to get over all my feelings right now. I have a right to be sad. I just lost my *abba*."

Esther erupted with a burst of laughter. I was shocked. I had been completely honest with her and now she was laughing at me?

"Wow. You know something, Jacob," she said. "I believe that's just about the healthiest answer I've ever heard! Thank you for saying that."

I took a breath, and Esther smiled.

"If you prefer not to see a psychologist, how about if you and I meet together, just the two of us a few times?"

I wasn't sure. I instinctively trusted this woman, but I couldn't imagine myself talking openly to anyone about what was happening to me. How could I say those words? She recognized my hesitation.

"We don't have to talk about anything you don't want to talk about, Jacob. You're in charge. You can trust me," she said with a smile.

And I did.

I met with Esther regularly for almost a year — and it turned out to be one of the best decisions of my life. We spoke a lot about the family, who we were and how we related to each other. I talked about my father. I told her about my fears and how terrified I was of the future. And we spoke a great deal about my dreams, especially my nightmares. I felt completely comfortable with Esther and grateful to know that whatever happened during my week, I could share it with her.

Of course, my time with Esther didn't give me back the life I had before the murder — nothing ever could. I still missed my father with an intensity of pain and love that threatened to pour out of me in sobs at any time in any place — and did. I still plodded through my classes and schoolwork without any real interest or attention, pushed forward only by my mother's support and the promise I had made to my father. My nightmares would still exhaust me and haunt me for days. I could still unexpectedly be transported back to the sights and sounds of the attack with such force that it could, quite literally, take my breath away.

But during that year, Esther became a conduit through which I could see the tiniest glimmer of a future for myself that wasn't wholly defined by pain. And, perhaps even more importantly, she assured me that what I was feeling was normal, a normal response to what I had been through.

"I'm telling you I was lying down in the cemetery on my father's grave, touching his name and that it felt good to me," I told her one day. "I was happy to be there, happy to be lying on a grave. Are you telling me that's normal? How can that be normal?"

"It's normal because that's what people do when they're in pain, Jacob. Because when someone you love so much is ripped away from your life, people find solace wherever they can." She smiled at me. "Do you think you're the first person who ever went to lie down on the grave of a loved one?"

"I don't know. I've never heard of anyone doing that. Ever."

"Of course you haven't," she said gently. "But do you know why you haven't? Because people don't talk about it. They do it, Jacob. I promise you. They just don't talk about it."

"So I guess I'm not the only one who does these weird things?" I smiled at her.

She looked at me with a serious face and said, "Jacob, some people write letters to their loved ones years and decades after they're gone," she said. "Did you know that? For some people, it's a comforting way to still feel connected. Some people still shop for birthday gifts for their loved one, or even go to the grave to eat a birthday dinner. Did you know that?"

"No."

"But they do. I promise you it's true. We're all human. And you're human, too. So it's OK that you have emotions you can't understand or control right now."

I shook my head and wiped my tears. It made me so sad

to hear her words. I imagined what it must be like for a parent to lose a child, to go to the cemetery with a stuffed animal or a birthday cake. I could imagine the letters people left on graves, the flowers and the tears that dried after sitting on the graves for hours under the sun.

"Remember when you told me you had a right to be sad because you'd just lost your precious *abba?* You were right. It's normal to feel as badly as you feel right now and to do the things you're doing for comfort. It's normal. And one day, I promise you, you will feel better than you do now. You will be stronger, Jacob. You'll be fine."

I heard her say I would be fine. At that time, I just couldn't see it.

But after many, many conversations, I did come to understand what Esther was telling me. Even living in a country where murder and death seemed to have become part of our very existence, we did not actually talk about grief and mourning. We fell back on our traditions without educating people about what to expect emotionally, about grief's many forms and how to get through the roller coaster of such a loss.

I was so blessed to work with Esther. She taught me that each person's grief was unique and personal and that there was no "right" way or "wrong" way to go through this journey. Esther never pushed me to "get over" my loss or to get back into the life I lived before the attack. She respected the fact that I wasn't yet ready to get beyond the raw wound of having lost my father. She understood that I wanted people to know I was a mourner for the same reason I hadn't wanted to shave my mourning beard or remove my black shirt — because I wanted everyone to know that my father was murdered as an innocent man, and I wanted everyone to know who killed him. I wanted them to know what a wonderful man he was. I was afraid that if everyone thought I was doing well, no one would remember what happened and all the murdered victims of terrorism would lose their voices forever. I could not let that be.

One of Esther's greatest concerns was my nightmares. We spoke about them at almost every session. One day she suggested again that I see a psychologist.

"I know you said 'no' the first time I mentioned it. But I'm concerned about the impact these dreams are having on you. I know a particular psychologist I really think could help."

But I told her no, I still felt a great sense of fear when I thought about discussing my emotions with a psychologist. I didn't want to go.

"But you don't mind coming to speak with me, right?"

At that, I had to smile. "Of course I don't mind."

"And you know you can trust me?"

"Of course."

"Then would you be willing to see him just one time? Just once, and then you can decide whether or not to continue." I agreed.

When I arrived at my appointment with the psychologist, I felt my entire body tense up just as it had when I first met Esther. We introduced ourselves and spoke for a few minutes. I discovered he had just moved to Israel from the U.S. a few years earlier and seemed like a genuinely nice person, and I relaxed just a bit. When he asked me to talk about my dreams, he seemed to understand how disturbing they were to me, how disruptive they were to my life. He listened carefully with respect and a kind demeanor. At the end of the session, he said he did think he would be able to help me and he looked forward to our time together. I thanked him and shook his hand.

"There's no way I'll ever see him again," I told Esther at our next meeting.

"All right. You said you'd go once and you did. Fair enough," she said. "But I'm just curious as to why you wouldn't see him again."

"Because he wants to get rid of my dreams, and I can't do that. If I get rid of my dreams, I'll never see my *abba* again. That's the only place I have to be with him. I hate the nightmares — of course I do! I hate what they do to me! But if I have to suffer through them in order to see my *abba*, then that's what I'm going to do," I said. "And no one is going to take that away from me!"

Esther nodded her head as we sat together in silence for a moment. Then she said, "You seem pretty angry about that, Jacob."

"I'm so frustrated!" I wiped my eyes. "Tired and frustrated. And scared." I blew my nose again. "I'm so tired of being in pain that I could scream."

Esther took a deep breath and then stood up. "That's a great thing to do."

"What?"

"Scream. I like to scream when I'm angry or frustrated."

"What?" I smiled in spite of myself. "You like to scream?"

"I sure do. It feels good."

I started laughing. "What kind of a social-work idea is that?"

"It's a good one," she said. "Come on, let's open the window and scream together."

"That's ridiculous. I can't do it."

"Sure you can."

"No, I really can't."

"You can't? You're telling me you're not able to scream? You don't know how to do it?" She shook her head and smiled as she reached her hand down to me. "Come on. Stand up. Let's scream."

"Really, no. I'm too embarrassed."

She reconsidered. "OK," she said, "but you don't mind if I scream just a bit, do you?"

"What?" I was smiling again. "Are you really going to do that?"

"Yes, I sure am."

"OK. Go ahead."

Esther walked over to the windows. Her office was on the third floor and faced out onto an open field. This tiny woman opened the windows as wide as she could, stuck her head out, took a deep breath, and let out one of the loudest screams I had ever heard.

"Whoa! What are you doing?" I asked. By that point, I was laughing out loud. "What is this?"

"I'm screaming," she said with a smile. "Can't you tell?"

She took a deep breath in and screamed again.

"Esther, I think someone is going to come banging on your door in two seconds!" I got up and walked over to the window.

"Just like I told you — it feels good."

I was so self-conscious standing with her at that window. I could feel my face turning red. The more she screamed, the more embarrassed I became. Who was listening to this? But Esther clearly didn't care one bit what anyone else would think.

Finally, I decided I might as well give it a try. I took a breath and out came a feeble little shout. Even I couldn't hear myself above Esther's voice.

Esther dipped her head in my direction and looked at me over the top of her glasses. "*That* was it? I think you can do better."

I found myself laughing again. But this time I took in all my breath and let out a loud, long, satisfying scream. Then

I did it again, louder than before. And again, even louder. It did feel good. I screamed again. And again. I went for ear-splitting screams. Screams that could be heard blocks away. Screams like ocean waves crashing themselves onto the rocks. Screams that could have been heard over the chaos at Abu Kabir or the sirens at the bomb site. Screams that hurt my throat. Over and over. Screams and screams that narrowed my focus to this window, this room, this sound, right here, right now, in my body.

A few months into my sessions with Esther, she asked if I would do her a favor. Of course, I would do almost anything for her. She told me she knew a teenager who had lost his father in a terrorist attack.

"He's about 15 years old, and his mother doesn't know what to do with him. He's just become wild. He won't listen to his mother. He won't do his schoolwork. He's out on the streets all the time. I wonder if you would agree to see him."

"See him? You mean like make an appointment to try to help him?"

"Oh, no. Nothing like that. I'm just asking you to hang out with him. Just to let him know he's not as alone as he thinks he is. Just to be with him." I wasn't sure what to expect from the meeting but I was excited. I felt a responsibility to try to help him, and it felt good.

I met with this student three or four times. We never studied together or did homework or anything that would have directly helped him in school. We just hung out, played soccer together, walked, and talked. I let him talk as much or as little as he wanted about what he had been through. And I shared with him about my loss, too.

I'll never really know if I made a difference in this boy's life. But I do know one thing: This was the very first time I tried to support someone who had lost a loved one to terrorism. It felt good to think I might have helped, even a little bit.

Not long afterward, Esther told me about a group she thought I might want to join. For some time, the government had been offering support groups for women who had lost their husbands in a terrorist attack. Now, the government was starting a similar four-month-long program for young adults who had lost a parent in an attack. Esther suggested that while I continue to see her, I also join this group. I had never heard of anything like that, and I had no idea what it would be like. But I was willing to give it a try.

My mother heard about the meetings from Esther and put me in contact with a young man named Shay. Shay's mother also participated in my mother's group meetings. Both Shay's father and uncle had been murdered by terrorists the same year as my father, and his mother and my mother are still very close friends today. Shay and I met on the day of the first group meeting and drove together to a government facility in Kfar Saba, a city in the center of Israel where the meeting was held. On the way there, we shared our stories and spoke about the feelings our family members were facing now every day. We realized right away that he and I understood some things about each other that none of our other friends really grasped, even though Shay and I had just met.

At the meeting place, other people slowly came in, about 15 of us all together. We stood around for a bit with some cookies and coffee. I felt so confused. Why was I standing there? Was it possible that I belonged in a group for people who had lost a parent? Every young person standing in that room — each of us looking just like anyone else you would see on a college campus or in a coffee shop — had lost a mother, a father, or even more family members from the same senselessness that had ripped my *abba* from my life.

Why? I felt such a deep sadness for all of them. I wanted to know all their stories and I knew I would, over time.

After 20 minutes or so, we sat down in a circle, all facing each other, each of us nervous, some even with our coffees visibly shaking. The leaders spoke about the conditions in Israel and what the government was hoping to accomplish with this new program. They told us the work of healing would not be easy, but that they were here to help us. Then the psychologist asked that we go around the circle, each of us telling our name and where we're from.

"Just tell us whatever else you'd like us to know about yourself, your parents, your family, what happened to you, anything. You're welcome to talk, to laugh, to cry — whatever you want," he said. "And if you don't want to say anything other than your name and town, that is fine, too. Whatever you feel like." So we went around in the circle with each person giving his or her name and hometown.

And that was it.

No one said another word. We sat in absolute silence for over an hour.

When the leaders suggested we take a break for more coffee and cookies, we practically jumped out of our chairs. At the break table, people talked a bit, smiled nervously, and spent a great deal of attention fixing their coffee.

But when we sat back down, no one said one word. Ninety more minutes of awkward silence — looking around the circle, staring at our feet, trying to figure out what was happening here — felt like an eternity. I was so embarrassed. Almost three hours after the meeting began, the psychologist spoke up.

"Well, that's it for today," he said. Everyone giggled nervously. "It's OK. The silence is a process, too. There's a lot that needs to be said. And no need to worry—it will happen when it will happen. We'll see you in two weeks."

Although I was so confused by what had just occurred, my mind was clear about one thing: I wanted to see these people again. I worried the group would be canceled because no one had spoken up. Or even if it wasn't officially canceled, maybe no one would show up next time.

But most of us were back two weeks later, although a few had dropped out. We greeted each other like old friends. After all, we had even more in common now than we had the previous meeting: How many people have shared the experience of sitting together in awkward silence for so many hours? We laughed nervously as we moved our chairs again into a circle.

Once again, not one word. Not one person spoke up.

I could practically feel the tragedies that had brought us to this point in our lives hanging right above our heads, but no one — including me — wanted to be the first to reach up and acknowledge them. With the exception of our coffee break, we sat in complete silence for two and a half hours. Two and a half hours! That is a lot of silence.

But at the end of the meeting, the psychologist once again assured us that everything was moving along just fine, just as it needed to. He seemed completely comfortable and relaxed in the silence. I had never seen anything like it. Again, I worried that the group would be canceled.

We were down to about eight or nine people by the third time we met. But this time, there was no silence. This time, we spoke aloud the words we had previously been afraid to say. I talked about my pain and loss, the way I missed my father, the terrible fear I had about the future. I listened to my new friends speak about their families, their own nightmares, the empty holes in their homes, their personal horror. We talked and talked for two and a half hours. The more we talked, the more I recognized my new friends' stories. These were the families I had seen on the television news and read about in the newspapers. These were the young people I had seen standing at the graves, crying, in such pain — the generation from whom terrorism has taken so much.

When the session ended and the psychologist spoke to us, we could all see the happiness on his face. We realized we had moved into a new stage of our grief, a new stage of healing as we shared the horror of our losses and the trauma still inside us. But now that we had begun, we didn't want to stop. Spontaneously, we all went across the street to a coffee house and spent another two and a half hours together.

The psychologist who told us we could be comfortable with the silence and modeled that himself was such a wise man. He gave us the gift of time, time for our voices and our stories to rise from the silence exactly as they needed to.

What a blessing it was to spend time with these people who knew me and understood me and weren't afraid of their emotions or mine. What an opportunity to get to know people at the deepest level of their souls. I looked forward to these group meetings like I looked forward to nothing else at that time in my life. Yes, the government had set a time limit of four months for the group, but that didn't stop us from continuing to see each other. We would talk for hours and hours. Whenever we felt the need to take a break from our serious discussions, all we had to do was bring up the awkward silence from our first two meetings. We would laugh every time.

For me, this group became the miracle that gave me my life back. With the support of these wonderful people and what I was learning from Esther, I was able to open up and let out some of the poison that had filled my soul.

No, I would never again have the wholeness I had taken

for granted when my father was alive. I would never be that person again — strong and secure with every single thing I needed or wanted, and more. But the support and strength we gave each other in this group allowed me to believe that the sun could rise and shine on a new chapter in my life — a chapter that could be meaningful and fulfilling and loving in its own right.

I had found the beginning of my new sunrise.

CHAPTER TEN

A New Family

With Esther's help, the survivors group support, the love of my friends, encouragement from my dean, and my mother as the constant wind beneath my wings, I earnedmy bachelor's degree in October 2004.

My mother and Pazit came with me to the graduation ceremony, a beautiful celebration in a big hall with a band playing and all the traditional speeches. Students were called up one by one to receive their diploma and shake the dean's hand. It was a time for hugs and kisses, big smiles and family pictures. But all I felt was lonely and sad, and I think my mother and Pazit felt the same way, too. This was a huge accomplishment, a joyous occasion, and yes, they were proud of me. But all the happiness and celebration going on around us just served to point out that my father was not there. Where was my father at a time like this? It was almost unbearable to look around and see all the fathers beaming with pride and hugging their graduates. I could see the sadness in my mother's face, in my sister's face and later even in the photos we took.

Not long afterward, I went to the cemetery. I sat on my father's grave for several hours, holding the diploma I had promised to bring home to him. My parents — neither of whom had had the opportunity to attend college — had always stressed the importance of my education, and I knew my father would have been so proud of me. I spoke to him, I sat with him. I ran my hand across his name, comforted again by seeing the familiar letters. It felt good to be there. This time, I could enjoy the peace I felt at my father's grave without worrying that I had lost myself. I sat on the grave, closed my eyes, and rested.

. . .

Toward the end of my senior year, there had been a big push at school for students to continue their education beyond the bachelor's degree, and many universities came to speak to us about their programs. Although I hadn't previously thought about continuing my schooling, I found myself enthralled with the one-year master's program in management offered by Polytechnic New York in Rehovot, close to my home. This particular program was publicized all over Israel at the time, with ads emphasizing its benefits for students who might want to live and work abroad one day. We heard over and over how many executives would be joining the program and what a great opportunity it would be for networking. Although I had no plans to work abroad, I was attracted by the program's exciting four-quarter curriculum. When I spoke to my mother about it, she was very encouraging. At the school's informational meeting, I found I loved the people and the challenging syllabus.

I applied to the program and was accepted. I also applied for, and received, a scholarship from OneFamily Fund, a non-profit addressing the needs of those who had lost a loved one in a terrorist attack.

Classes began in January 2005. I had never enjoyed school the way I did during those first two quarters of my master's program. I absolutely loved it. The progress I had made in my personal healing allowed me to better focus in the classroom. The material we learned — most of which was printed in English, although we spoke in Hebrew — was fascinating to me. The professors and my classmates were engaging and stimulating. The students' average age was 45, and most were already managers, vice presidents, and CEOs dedicated to increasing their knowledge and skills. Just being involved with such accomplished people and benefiting from their wisdom and experience was an opportunity in itself.

I was so grateful for this experience that I wanted to thank OneFamily in person for my scholarship. Immediately after second-quarter exams in early summer 2005, I went to the organization's headquarters in Jerusalem. Along with my thanks, I brought a bouquet of flowers for director Chantal Belzberg.

Although I hadn't anticipated saying too much more than a "thank you," I spoke with Chantal for an hour and a half. I began the conversation feeling very self-conscious and embarrassed since we spoke only in English. But the longer we spoke, the more I focused on this wonderful organization and the less I worried about my accent or grammar.

It was Chantal's daughter, Michal, who had actually started OneFamily. On Michal's 12th birthday, a suicide bomber had murdered seven children and eight adults at a crowded pizzeria and injured another 130. Michal had been preparing for her bat mitzvah at the time, and she went ahead with the religious ceremony. However, she canceled her bat mitzvah party and contributed those expenses to the victims of the attack. She asked anyone who would have given her a gift to donate those funds, too. With Michal's efforts, the

Belzbergs raised quite a bit of money that week. But when they realized how much more was really needed to address the suffering, OneFamily was born.

Chantal spoke that day about OneFamily's work — how much had been accomplished and how much was still left to do. The fundraising itself was a never-ending job, she said, as the need was overwhelming. She asked about my own family, my mother, Moshe, Pazit, how everyone was managing. And when she asked how I was doing emotionally, I answered her honestly. I told her I missed my father with a terrible, deep ache every single day, but that I felt my life was slowly getting back on track with the help I had received from therapy and the support group. I thanked her again for OneFamily's support for my education.

"Jacob, I so appreciate your coming here to thank us in person. I really do. And the flowers are beautiful," she said, smiling. "But I wonder if there's something else you could do for us. In a few months, we're sending a group of survivors to the U.S. for three weeks to talk to people about what's really going on here in Israel. We've done this several times with great success. The best way for us to raise money to help the survivors is for people to hear directly what it's really like and what's really needed. I'd like to send you with this group, Jacob. Would you be willing to go?"

"Absolutely." I didn't hesitate for a second. "It would be an honor to deliver this message to my brothers and sisters across the ocean, and to tell my father's story." I was thrilled, as was my mother when I told her about it.

Our OneFamily survivors' group met once during the summer before our departure. We were 15 victims of terrorism who had lost children, parents, spouses, or siblings or been physically injured ourselves. We were young and old, from all parts of Israel, all backgrounds, all vocations. It was difficult to hear so many sad stories, to hear about so much hardship and loss. But I was inspired by their resiliency and the toughness in their eyes, and, of course, I loved the opportunity to tell everyone about my father. It was good to be with a group of survivors once again, to connect with people who shared my experience. As with my original support group, I realized these individuals offered me a level of empathy no one else could match. But equally importantly, if not more so, I saw in their eyes that I gave the same to them.

Chantal shared an amazing itinerary with us that day. We would be hosted in homes and speak in New York; New Jersey; Pennsylvania;, Washington, D.C.; Virginia; and Florida. We would meet with former New York City Mayor Rudy Giuliani and current Mayor Michael Bloomberg, in addition to business and Jewish community leaders in each city. I was so excited and honored to be a part of this. I began reading everything I could find about Giuliani, Bloomberg and the Jewish community in the States to prepare myself for the trip.

In August 2005, we began our journey by traveling to New York City with several OneFamily leaders. We were shocked to be greeted at the airport by a group of people who had been waiting just for us! That greeting made us feel so welcomed and loved. I'm not sure they ever understood how much their enormous smiles and their "cheerleading" meant to us — our wounded group, some of us visiting another country for the very first time, all of us in various stages of healing.

Our first meeting was held the very next day at a Jewish center in New York City with about 150 people in attendance. Our leaders asked for one or two of us to come forward to speak. I had never spoken in English in front of a group and I also knew that speaking for OneFamily held a tremendous responsibility. I was just too scared and shy to speak at that first meeting. But within a few days, I was coming forward to share my story. Sometimes several of us spoke at a particular venue, sometimes just one. Some of the survivors who shared their stories frequently in the early part of our trip didn't have the emotional energy to continue. In fact, by the end of the trip, there were only a few of us who still were able to serve as speakers. I, too, was tired. But I was so grateful for OneFamily and knew the need back home was so great that I felt compelled to push myself to share more and more.

Fairly early in the trip, we met with Giuliani at his office in the Empire State Building. As soon as he stepped into the room, I had the strange sensation that I was reconnecting with an old friend. Not only had I read his biography and so many news clippings, but like millions around the world, I felt he had been in our living room on 9/11. We all had hung on his every word that day, impressed by his leadership and the tremendous care he had shown for his citizens.

We sat with Giuliani around a very long table with city councilmen, rabbis, and the OneFamily leadership. He asked us to go around the table and each tell our stories. He wanted every detail, the names, the places, the ages — he wanted it all. You could see on his face that he had such compassion for us and our families, even though we had been strangers to him just moments before.

When it was my turn, I was so honored to know that Rudy Giuliani, a man my father had admired so greatly, had now heard the name of Rami Kimchy. I also told him that I knew he, too, had been through such pain and loss.

"When we sat as a family in Israel in our living room and watched the towers come down on 9/11, we were with you," I told him. "We felt it so strongly. We were all together that day, you and all of Israel, all of us. As victims of terrorism, we are all one family."

"Thank you," he said. And he nodded. "Jacob, tell me, how is your mother doing?"

"My mother is my superhero, Mr. Giuliani," I said. "She is just so strong. She has rooms that she cries in, but she will never show us even one tear. She is working so hard to move forward with her life."

When we finished sharing our stories and feelings with him, he took the time to share his own journey with us. He was speaking about 9/11 when an assistant entered the room to tell him it was time to move on to his next meeting.

"Not yet," he said. And he turned back to our group.

It was clear from his words and demeanor that terrorism was not just a talking point to this man — this was personal. Not only had a terrorist attack torn apart his city and his country, but he had also lost a dear personal friend that day. He was speaking about his losses and his own path to healing when another assistant came in to tell him our time was up.

"Not yet," he said again.

Rudy Giuliani spent two and a half hours with our group that day, even though others were waiting for him. He took time to hug each of us, to smile at each of us, to take photos with us. He gave us so much love, inspiration, and strength that I could feel it in my body and my soul. I was so grateful.

Our trip also included a wonderful meeting with Michael Bloomberg. Mayor Bloomberg spoke to us about New York City and his insistence that terrorism will not define life for its citizens.

"Terrorism changed our city and it changed our country, but it will not win," he told us with such strength and conviction. "We will continue. The people will continue. *We* will win."

After the mayor spoke, most of our group spread out to take pictures of the beautiful City Hall building and artwork. But a few of us had the opportunity to speak with him more personally. We talked about the relationship between the U.S. and Israel and the Jewish community in New York City. I left that meeting feeling so inspired, stronger than I had before.

Marc Belzberg, Chantal's husband, joined the trip the night we met at the home of Len Leader, former CFO of AOL, president of AOL Time Warner's corporate venture investment group, and a wonderful Jewish philanthropist. Marc traveled with us for several days, showing such love and support. He was so incredibly kind, always smiling, always helpful and patient, so sensitive to everyone's needs.

I had shared my story at Mr. Leader's house and at several others by that point in the trip, and was becoming more and more comfortable speaking in public. But when I stood up to speak in front of 800 people at a large New Jersey synagogue, I was terrified. Nothing had prepared me for such a large crowd! My heart was pounding so hard that I was sure everyone in the audience could see my suit jacket moving — ba-boom, ba-boom, ba-boom — like in a cartoon. I could barely swallow, and my hands were literally shaking. But somehow, I walked up to the podium and started to speak.

I described life in Israel with the constant bombings and murders. I told them about my father and the type of man he was, the reason he was in The Sheffield Club that night, and what had happened to him.

And then I stopped.

I was suddenly overcome by my emotions. My mouth was so dry I could barely move my tongue. And I was exhausted from the effort of speaking in English in front of such a large crowd.

The audience started to applaud. So I said, "Wait! I'm not done!"

At that, everyone in the room laughed, including me, and I finally relaxed a bit. These people had taken time out of their busy lives to come hear the stories of people they didn't know and would probably never see again. I wanted to make sure I gave them what they had come for — the truth about what was happening in Israel. I drank some water and continued to speak, more slowly and calmly this time.

When I finished and the applause stopped, more than 100 people stood in line to shake my hand and thank me. This was overwhelming! Me? I couldn't believe it. But these people were so wonderful. They hugged me and held me and shared with me that they had lost their brother in the 9/11 attack or their father or child. Some people told me they would double or even triple their donation based on what I had shared. And, as we had experienced so many times on this trip, these wonderful people shared their strength with us; we left that synagogue stronger than when we had arrived.

But it was at a home in New Jersey in front of a much, much smaller group that I gave the speech that was most important to me personally. We had been told that several people in the gathering that night had the ability to make significant financial contributions. I wondered how I could help them best understand how great the need was. How could I help them understand what Israelis were suffering through, what it was like to live with terrorism day in and day out? I decided to speak about what I had witnessed at the Sheffield Club — for the very first time.

Three years and three months had passed since my father's murder. During that time, I had spoken a great deal about my father, about terrorism in general, and about what his loss meant to me. But I had *never* described to anyone the details of what I had witnessed that night.

I hadn't initially planned to be silent for three years. But during the shiva period and immediately afterward, my family was in such pain that I couldn't consider adding to that pain by describing what I had seen. When I started meeting with Esther and the support group, I told them only that I had been at the scene of the attack. That was true as far as it went — and no one had pushed me for more. Maybe they felt that if I had needed to speak about it, I would have. Over time, I even stopped referring to the fact that I had been at the attack scene. In fact, some newer friends, even some who knew me quite well, had no idea I had even been at the site that night.

Of course, even if I had wanted to speak about it earlier on, I don't know how I could have. I don't know how my mouth could have formed the words.

As a younger person, I had seen so many movies or read books in which a character is questioned about a violent event but remains silent. I had always wanted to scream at the character, "Just say it! You have to say it!" Because in each case, it was clear that something sinister could be averted if the person would just speak up. But after my father's murder, those were the characters I related to most strongly; some things were just too difficult to say. Silence became my protection.

But there was another, even more significant reason for my silence: I simply had not understood how severely I had been traumatized and victimized by what I had witnessed that night. I understood that I was a victim of terrorism, unquestionably. But I believed I was a victim of terrorism because of one singular fact: my father had been murdered in a terrorist attack. I believed that one fact alone was the source of all my pain. Consequently, that's what I spoke about in my healing work with Esther and the group.

But I was terribly mistaken. The truth is that my mind

and heart also had been ripped apart by witnessing the most heinous that humanity has to offer.

What could be worse than a crime so violent it tears a human being's head off as easily as a child playing with a cheap plastic doll? A crime that shreds innocent people to non-recognizable bits? A crime that forces those who come to help to walk on and desecrate pieces of human flesh without even knowing it?

I understand now that no one could witness such evil without being emotionally sickened and scarred.

Just a few years ago in Israel, I started talking with a man I had just met. One thing led to another in our conversation, and he asked me about my father and how I had lost him. When I told him my father was a victim of the Sheffield Club suicide bombing, his eyes became huge and he sucked in his breath.

"I was there that night, too," he said. "I was working there." This man had been with ZAKA, the organization that comes to an attack site to pick up the tiny body parts others might overlook — fingers, ears, bits of bone, whatever they find — to make sure that even the smallest pieces of a human being are treated with appropriate dignity.

"But after the Sheffield Club bombing, I had to quit," he told me. "I had been doing that work for a while, but I had never seen, or even imagined, such a slaughter as what I saw that night. I have never forgotten what happened there."

That conversation confirmed to me that what I had witnessed was among the worst of the worst. And yet, I had not attached any value to its effect on me. In fact, I had buried that trauma deeper and deeper within myself as I focused only on the terrible grief of losing my father. But now, in New Jersey, at the home of a man I had just met, now it was time.

As I prepared myself to speak, I suddenly remembered

the question my friend from the intelligence service had asked me the night of the attack. Before she gave me the address of the attack, she had said, "Jacob, are you sure you're willing to be a witness to this crime?" I told her I was sure.

But had I ever really understood her question? What did it mean to be a witness? Did it mean keeping the truth buried deep within myself, year after year pushing it farther and farther down into my soul? Or was there a responsibility that came with bearing witness to such a crime? I also remembered how hard I had struggled that night to keep my focus. I could have so easily allowed myself to run from what I saw or even collapse into unconsciousness on the street. But I fought against that. Why? Had I forced myself to see and smell and hear this evil just to keep silent about it?

I took several slow, deep breaths to calm myself.

"As you know, OneFamily has been touring the States for a couple of wonderful weeks now, and many of us in this group of survivors have shared our personal stories," I began. "But what I need to tell you tonight is something I have never shared with these amazing new friends, or with our wonderful leaders — not even with my mother. I have never spoken of this with anyone. But this is what you need to know in order to really understand the evil that is ripping out the heart of our country."

And I spoke. I didn't say very much. I didn't describe too many details. But I did say more of the truth than they had ever heard and more of the truth than I had ever spoken aloud. It was very, very difficult for me, but it was a beginning. I had opened up another new place inside my soul. I had allowed another bit of the poison out and made room for a new bit of light to enter.

I believe that exact type of healing — slowly letting a bit of the poison out to make room for the light — was something all 15 of us experienced on that journey. Each time we spoke, each time we met with a new group of people who gave us love by taking time to learn about our lives, each time we shared our stories among ourselves, a little bit of healing took place. As we prepared to leave the States to go back home, we each felt a bit stronger, a bit healthier, more loved, and more capable of facing the challenges in our own lives.

I was so struck by the way our lives had all changed for the better in such a short time! This trip had been one of the most positive experiences of my life. So powerful, so positive in fact, that my only thought was to share it with others, to *give* it to others for the sake of their own healing. On the long flight back to Israel, I asked myself question after question. How could I share this experience beyond OneFamily? How could I help make this same difference in the lives of others? How could I do that in Israel? But what about victims of terrorism in other places — Ireland, England, Spain, France? How could I help them, too? I felt I had been shown a great, almost magical, prescription for healing. How could I not share that with as many people as possible, as quickly as possible?

My mother greeted me at the airport, and we hugged each other tightly. I had missed her so much, it was wonderful to be in each other's arms again. I was thrilled to be home.

And yet, a few days later, after I had rested up and worked through some of the answers to my questions, I told my mother I needed to talk to her.

"*Ima*," I said looking straight into her eyes, "there's something I need to do and I need to do it now. *Ima*, I need to go to New York to establish a non-profit to support victims of terrorism. I know I can do this, and I feel I must do it now."

My mother raised her eyebrows.

"Jacob," she said gently, still holding my eyes with her steady gaze, "you're crazy."

CHAPTER ELEVEN
Finding One Heart

Of course my mother thought I was crazy!

I was in the very middle of my master's degree, and she knew I loved the program. I had already received one very lucrative job offer — and had every reason to believe I would receive others after finishing the degree — which my mother also knew. From time to time, I had thought about the possibility of living outside Israel for the experience of learning about another culture, but I hated being away from my mother, as well as my brother, sister, my niece and nephew, and all my aunts, uncles and cousins. Not to mention my many, many friends. And now, I come home from a three-week trip and want to turn all that upside down and completely change my life? Of course she thought I was crazy.

It's all we talked about when I got home.

"Why can't you just stay in Israel, continue school, and start your life after that? Like my friends whose children go to school, get married, have children of their own, enjoy a good job, a good life. Doesn't that sound good to you? Is something wrong with that?"

"Nothing is wrong with that. It sounds great, *ima*. It really does," I said. "But something is telling me I have to do it

— to go back to New York and change the world as much as I can. I came back from the OneFamily trip with this special energy, so much desire and power and confidence. I know I need to go back there to start my new path in life. I want to help as many victims as I can.

"*Ima*, I wish you could have seen what happened on this trip. We touched people's hearts by sharing our stories, and as we did, we became stronger, too. There was one guy in our group who had lost his sister to an attack only days before we left for New York. How he even made it on the trip, I have no idea. But even he experienced some healing from the talking, from the sharing, from the unique support that only survivors can give to each other. Sadly, you know exactly what I'm talking about."

"Jacob . . . "

The next day, we were in the kitchen making dinner together.

"I know this is hard for you to understand because it's happening so fast, all at once," I told her. "And because you know I don't really want to be away from you and everyone else here."

"So why do you have to go to New York? Why can't you do it here?"

"Because I want to unite victims from around the world. To offer help to all of them. And I believe that such an organization should be based in New York City. New York City is like the center of the world."

We chopped vegetables in silence for a bit.

"I have this vision, such a strong passion, to help Jews, Muslims, and Christians. To help people from different religions and backgrounds, to break down the walls between us and to create understanding, peace, and friendship. All of us live in this one world together, and so many of us are suffering. We need to hug and support each other."

We continued with our coffee the next morning.

"Can't you at least wait until you finish your degree? If this new program you want to create is such a great idea now, why won't it still be a great idea in six months? Why don't you just finish your degree? Six months from now, with your master's degree in your hand, you can think about it again."

"I just don't want to wait. I feel the voice inside of me telling me to do it now."

My mother took a deep breath and shook her head. "Jacob . . . "

She knew I was serious.

"Do you remember what *Abba* always used to say to me? What he said to me when I was just a little boy so terrified of getting in the swimming pool?"

She didn't answer.

"He said it to me over and over again, so many times in my life. 'Jacob, never be afraid of anything. There is nothing you cannot do. Nothing.' Do you remember that? It's *Abba* who gave me the strength and courage to know that I could do anything I put my mind to. Anything. And this? This is my mission in my life now, *Ima*. And I will do it all in memory of Rami Kimchy."

"Jacob." She shook her head again and just looked at me. I thought I saw the beginning of tears . . . and a smile.

I gave her a big smile in return. "*Ima*, please. Come let's have a hug. You know how much I love you."

My mother is such a smart woman. From the very beginning, she knew I wasn't asking for her permission — because we both knew I didn't need it. I was asking only for her blessing, which she gave me in that hug.

"Just do me one favor, Jacob, please."

"What's that?"

"Just go to your school and tell them your plans, and make sure you can still get your degree. Please. At least do that much."

I went to see the director of the program later that week and told him I was going to New York City to open a non-profit in memory of my father. I explained about the support groups.

"I think it sounds like a wonderful career path for you, Jacob," he said with a genuine smile. "And your degree will help with non-profit management. It will definitely give you more credibility with funders, although that's not the direction most of our students take."

"Actually, I'm leaving very soon."

"What do you mean, 'very soon?'"

"I plan to leave in the next few weeks. I'll miss part of the program, but I would still like to do the work and earn my degree. I'm hoping there's a way we can work that out," I said.

"You want to leave before the program is over and still earn your degree?"

"No. I don't *want* to leave the program. I love the classes, the professors, the other students. I don't want to give that up, but I just don't have a choice," I told him. "I've decided to start building this foundation to help the victims now. I'm getting ready to book my flight."

"You have to do it right now?" he asked. He could hardly believe what I was saying.

"Yes. I do."

The director leaned back in his chair. We stared at each other in silence for a bit, neither of us looking away.

Eventually he took a few deep breaths, cleared his throat and said, "OK, here's what I can do for you, Jacob. We'll give you all the materials. You can take everything with you, and we'll send you whatever additional materials you'll need. But you'll have to learn it completely on your own. And you'll have to come back to Israel to take all exams with your classmates. That's it."

"All right. Could I take the exams at your New York campus since I'll be right there in the city?"

"No. You can't. You started here at our Israel campus and if you want that degree, you'll fly back to Israel to take your exams here. That's it. That's the offer." He stood up to dismiss me. "You have a difficult decision to make, Jacob. Take some time to think about it."

"I don't need more time to think about it," I said, standing up and reaching across the desk to shake his hand. "Thank you so much, sir. I appreciate what you're willing to do for me. I accept the responsibility of coming back to Israel to take the exams."

My mother was relieved to hear my news. "You be sure to get yourself back here for those exams," she said. "And just for the record, I still think you're crazy." But this time, she said it with a smile.

. . .

A few weeks later, my plane touched down in New York City. I was thrilled!

I knew very few people in the city, didn't know where I would live, wasn't exactly sure how to accomplish my goals, and didn't know how long it would take me to put an organization together. But those were just details. The only thing that mattered to me was my mission, my purpose. I heard my father's words at my back, pushing me forward: "There's nothing you can't do." I felt like one huge bundle of positive energy, and I'm not sure my feet touched the ground as I walked out of the airport.

Staying with friends I had met on the OneFamily trip until I moved into my own apartment, I immediately began networking. I met with the few people I knew, then with their contacts, and *their* contacts. I met with anyone who would listen to my plans, give me advice, or donate to this cause. So many people were encouraging, always willing to listen, to brainstorm with me and offer support. I was amazed by the generosity of those who offered to donate office space, computers, airline miles, meeting space, so many things we would need.

But who *were* we? This organization needed a name.

We needed a name that said being victimized by terrorism felt the same in Israel as it did in Ireland, as it did in Madrid, as it did in New York City. A name that said we suffer together because we are all human beings — and we can open our hearts and heal together, too. A name that would have made my father proud, since it would be forever dedicated to his memory.

One Heart Global was born.

Together with some wonderful new friends I'd met on the OneFamily mission, we founded an organization with a global vision to help victims of terrorism from around the world.

I kept my promise to my mother and flew back to Israel for all my exams. Although I certainly missed my classmates and professors, I never doubted my decision, and had no trouble passing my exams. I earned my master's degree in January 2006. Instead of attending a graduation ceremony this time, I joined a small ceremony in Brooklyn where the same director who had given me permission to move to New York now handed me my diploma.

On one of my next trips to Israel, I took my new diploma to the cemetery. Again I sat on my father's grave, enjoying the comfort of being "with" him. Although my father was with me every single day and always would be — whether in New York or Israel or anywhere else in this world — I did feel a special comfort at his grave. And I was able to accept that for what it was.

One night over dinner, I shared a fundraising idea with my mother.

"*Ima*, what do you think about me trying to sell Israeli art in New York?"

"You mean as a representative for the artists? To make money as an agent?"

"No, no. I don't want to formally represent them," I said. "I want to just ask them to donate some artwork and then I can sell it to benefit One Heart Global."

My mother raised her eyebrows at me, an expression of her skepticism I had by now seen many times.

"Really? And where are you going to find Israeli artists willing to donate their work for a project that benefits people in New York City?" she asked. "Don't you think Israeli artists will assume New York City has enough money without their help?"

"I hadn't thought of that," I admitted. "But I won't really know the answer until I talk to the artists."

People had been very generous in donating all types of items and services to One Heart in New York. But of course any organization also needs cash. Several people who had promised to make a financial contribution had never followed through on those promises. I was new to the non-profit world, so I didn't realize that this was not altogether uncommon. What I did realize was that I needed to raise money, a part of my job as organizational co-founder that was completely new to me.

"And suppose you do get a few paintings or sculptures donated here for you to sell in New York. Jacob, do you have any idea how much it could cost to ship those things?"

"Good point. No, I don't," I answered. "But I'll find out."

We ate in silence for a bit.

I was naïve and excited, both of which showed as I continued to talk with my mother about my idea. I had some acquaintances who knew some artists, and I imagined it would be easy for me to get support by networking like that.

"I don't think you will get any donation from artists," my mother said. "But this is just my opinion."

It certainly wasn't easy to hear that, but it didn't keep me from moving ahead with the project. I decided to reach out to as many artists as possible as quickly as possible. Online, I found information about 15 artists and emailed each of them. I told them who I was, about my background, my father's murder, about One Heart and about the art show I had in mind. The response was absolutely astonishing, much greater than anything I had even hoped for. Within weeks, word of mouth and networking had led to 85 amazing artists donating a total of 180 pieces of artwork — jewelry, paintings, sculptures, and more. I was in shock. My mother was so proud. I felt like I was in the movie "Mission Impossible."

But once I had driven all over Israel to pick up the art and I began calculating the cost of shipping it to New York, I discovered my mother had been right. The retail costs of shipping would have been prohibitive. Again, I decided to ask for donations. I called all the big international freight companies, and I called and I called. And every single company turned me down flat. What was I going to do? Finally, I turned to a family-owned Israeli company. After days of getting the run-around within that company, I decided to email the CEO directly. I explained who I was, the mission of One Heart Global, and the help I needed. What did I have to lose?

I was shocked to receive an email back almost immediately — with an apology. "Dear Jacob, I am so sorry for what you have been through. My company will not only be happy to help you with your mission, but I am personally taking on this project myself. You have nothing to worry about. We will not only ship the artwork for you at no charge, but we'll make sure it is professionally wrapped, and we'll take care of releasing it from customs. Thank you for what you are doing on behalf of victims of terrorism."

I was absolutely overwhelmed by this man's generosity and kindness. He offered to take care of issues I hadn't even known to anticipate! It would have been so easy to give up. But I'm so glad I decided to keep at it — an important lesson for me and everyone else, no matter what we are trying to achieve. But in addition, clearly something in the mission of One Heart Global had touched him deeply. And I was more grateful than I could say.

So now, I had the artwork and I would have it all shipped to New York at no charge. But where would I hold the fund-raising event? I began to call various locations specifically in the Jewish community and was shocked to learn that no one would donate the space. Even one of the Jewish centers in New York City wanted to charge $2,000 for us to lease the space for only four hours. And that was the *least* expensive location we could find — but I just didn't see how it made sense to pay $2,000.

I left Israel and flew back to New York not knowing what I would do. Since I can never sleep on these long flights between Israel and the States, I found myself walking up and down the aisle thinking about this question. Before long, I realized that one of the women on the flight looked very familiar to me. After walking up and back a few more times, I realized she was looking at me, as well.

"I'm so sorry to interrupt you, but I think I know you from somewhere," I said to her on my next pass by her seat.

"And I feel the same way." She told me her name was Rachel and she lived in New York, but it took me a while to place her.

"Oh my goodness, do you own a spa?" I asked her.

"Yes, why?" She gave me the name of the spa. "Have you been there?"

"Did you host a group of terrorism survivors with an organization called OneFamily? Did you donate a free massage for each person to help them relax?"

That was it. She had been so kind as to donate a massage for each person on our trip, and I certainly had remembered her kindness. She had spent a lot of time with our group, shared so many smiles, and spoken to each person.

"I even have a photo of you with our group!" I told her.

As we talked, I told her how the OneFamily trip had changed my life, about my move to New York and the establishment of One Heart Global. I told her about our mission, my excitement, and then about our challenges. I still had the Jewish center on my mind and the $2,000 charge.

"Can you come to my office next week?" she asked me.

"Sure, of course. I'd love to talk to you again." I always love making a new friend, learning about new people, but I knew so few people in New York at that time that I was even more excited.

"I'd love to talk to you again, too, Jacob," she said with a smile. "But more than that, I'd like to write you a check for the $2,000. You're raising funds so you can help others who are in tremendous need. And I want to be a part of that." I was absolutely overwhelmed.

With Rachel's help, the shipping company, the many artists who donated work, and the Israeli Deputy Consul

General who spoke to support One Heart Global, we held our first, and very successful, fundraiser in New York. Mission Accomplished!

. . .

In February 2006, I booked a short break to visit a girl I knew in Florida. But New York was experiencing a record-breaking snowstorm at the time, and when I got to the airport, I discovered my flight would be delayed for eight hours. While I was waiting, I called my mother to catch up. Afterward, a man sitting near me turned to me and said, "Shalom." He was a young Israeli traveling around the States and also stranded at the airport that day. We began chatting in Hebrew, and I told him that if he would save my seat — the airport was so crowded it was hard to even find a seat — I would go buy some fruit and snacks for us to share.

When I came back, a woman who had been sitting near us also greeted me with "Shalom." And then she handed me a newspaper article.

"Read it," she said.

I looked at the newspaper and was shocked to realize the article was about victims of terrorism.

"How did you know?" I asked her.

"How did I know what?" she asked.

"How did you know that I help these people?"

Of course, she hadn't known. But she had overheard me speaking in Hebrew and was aware of the terrorism in Israel. She said she was a psychologist who helped victims of terrorism as well.

As we chatted, I told her a bit more about myself and One Heart Global, and I spoke about the loss of my father. I could see her face become very serious as I continued to tell her more of what my family had been through. When I finished talking, I took my father's picture out of my wallet.

"Look at this smile. That was my father," I said.

"And now, I will share my story," she said as she took a picture out of her own wallet. The photo was a picture of her only son, killed 12 years earlier in a car accident a few months before his bar mitzvah.

Here we were, two complete strangers brought together at the airport by a massive snowstorm. And now, having known each other for only a matter of minutes, we were sharing the most important facts of our lives — a loss that we instinctively knew the other person would respect. We both felt this was a friendship that was meant to be.

My new friend, Barbara Chasen, Ph.D., was not just a wonderful person; she was a psychoanalyst whose work focused, in part, on grief recovery. We saw each other again as soon as we both returned to New York. When I told her more about my vision for One Heart, she said she wanted to become involved.

"I would love to have your help and your professional expertise," I told her. "We definitely need a therapist to work with us."

"Jacob, please let me help," she said. "I would love to volunteer."

We had a long list of programs and services we wanted One Heart Global to provide. But I wanted to begin by establishing a support group since the terror victims' support group had been so vital to my own healing. Being in New York, we decided to reach out to the many victims of 9/11 I felt sure had never spoken about their trauma. I knew they were suffering — the sisters and brothers, parents, children, spouses, grandparents, as well as those who might not have known any of the murdered, but who lived through the terror of watching people jump to their deaths as the city crumbled around them.

We reached out to the World Trade Center Survivors' Network, an organization that had been established soon after 9/11 by a group of survivors who found each other online. The Network offered a variety of services, educational programs, and conferences, and represented the survivors' interests with respect to a memorial museum and redevelopment of the site. They were excited to collaborate with us in forming our support groups. We decided to call the groups "Survivors' Circles."

One Heart Global's Survivors' Circles began meeting in June 2006, eight months after my arrival in New York. I felt absolutely overwhelmed as I looked around the room that evening at Barbara and the dozen or so participants. I knew this was just the beginning of my work on behalf of terrorism survivors. But at the same time, I felt I had already accomplished my mission. Just bringing these survivors together was everything to me, because I knew *that* was the key. I knew first-hand the amazing healing that could happen just by talking. Or even by sitting together quietly. It was exactly how I had envisioned it.

Barbara explained that no one was required to share their story and that each person was welcome to just sit quietly if they wanted to. We did not sit through two and a half hours of silence that night, but if we had, I would have been just fine with it. I completely trusted the process, and the evening was extraordinary.

Knowing that I had accomplished this much was an overwhelming feeling. With my cofounders and Barbara, we managed to build the same support-group program that the State of Israel had offered to me. But that program took an entire government to build — and here I was, just a 28-year-old guy, living in a foreign country, working so hard with my cofounders, putting our pure hearts and souls into this program. As I sat in that first Survivors' Circle, I felt the sky was the limit for One Heart, for me. There were so many, many ways in which I wanted to help. I absolutely knew more good would come from our efforts.

Just one month after our first Survivors' Circle meeting, in July 2006, the Second Lebanon War broke out in Israel. How could I stay in New York, knowing how many children and families were being traumatized back home? I knew my own family and friends were all safe, for now. But for the thousands living in the north, closer to Lebanon, every day was a nightmare. These poor children spent hours every day in the bomb shelters, day after day, sometimes for days at a time.

I spoke to a psychologist to better appreciate the children's needs so I could understand the best way to make a real difference. She suggested we give them something they could physically hold in their hands while they're underground — a small, soft toy for each child to take into the shelter when the sirens go off.

One Heart Global immediately went to work. We organized a huge fundraiser in New York and New Jersey for toys and other items the families might need in a bomb shelter. People were so generous. I had planned to take the toys back to Israel with me, but people had donated much more than any few people could take on a plane. We shipped boxes of toys, and I took as much as I could with me on the plane, as well.

When I got to Israel and since we didn't know how long the war would last or whether the children would be out of the bomb shelters before school started, I collected backpacks, school supplies, and candies, and put the toys we collected into the packs, too. I drove north to Kiryat Shmona, just a few miles from Lebanese border, and brought dozens of bags to the city hall. But then I also drove directly to the local villages, some of which were even closer to the border. This was not a particularly safe thing to do — and I certainly didn't tell my mother where I was going — but I had to make sure the One Heart bags were placed directly into the hands of the children who needed them.

In the middle of a war in such a dangerous area, people were not used to seeing strangers drive up with gifts.

"Who are you? What are you doing here?"

I heard that many times and I could certainly understand their suspicions. But as soon as I explained that One Heart had come to help, I was welcomed. I saw the children delighted with their new bags, toys, pencils, and paper, and I knew the next time the siren sounded and they ran to the shelter, they would have a bit more comfort there. I felt no fear being in such a dangerous area because I was completely energized by my desire to listen to people's needs and to support them as much as I could.

Not all children were sheltered near their homes, however. We started to hear disturbing stories of children as young as 8 years old whose parents had sent them to friends and families in the center of Israel away from the dangerous northern border. Where were all these children? Who was taking care of them?

After speaking with various agencies and doing as much research as I could, I located groups of children staying at community centers. I drove to every location I could find, bringing the gift bags with me. I also spoke to every child I could find, telling them how strong they were, encouraging them to keep faith that they would be safe and secure, back with their families soon. I told them that terrorism will never win. I wanted to make sure they understood and thought that way as well. I did whatever I could to help them.

But perhaps the most important and heart-wrenching work we did was with a group of special-needs children who had come to my hometown to wait out the war. An organization had brought them down from the north with their parents' consent and somehow managed to care for them all. Some of the children in wheelchairs could not function on their own at all. Some could barely speak. Others had some mobility and good mental functioning. But whatever their level of ability, we just wanted them to feel cared for — even in a setting that was so different from what they were used to and without the people they loved most. I can hardly imagine how difficult and lonely that separation must have been for them. These children brought to my heart the group of disabled individuals I had volunteered with near my home after I finished my military service. I hoped they were safe and sound and well cared for now, too.

One Heart organized a huge party for these children, just before the beginning of Shabbat one week. We gave them bags filled with goodies and we had live music for them to dance to, move to, or enjoy in whatever way they could. It brought us so much joy to give them a moment of happiness. There is just nothing like that feeling.

I also worked in the south of Israel that summer, on another project I kept from my mother. Every day, missiles were being fired into southern Israel from Hamas in Gaza. And every day, Palestinians got on TV to say it wasn't true. But we knew children and adults were being terrorized by these missiles — and that the terror was real.

One local police station in the south of Israel had amassed hundreds and hundreds of these missiles, literally dragging them across the landscape to gather them at one place. When I heard about that, I knew I had to get the word out to every contact we had in the States, to let them know what was really happening. I went to that location with another volunteer to photograph every missile we could see that had been fired into Israel. We took picture after picture, from every single angle. Two local students also volunteered their time and talents by donating copies of missile photos they took previously.

The missiles didn't stop coming while we were there; one person was killed less than two miles from our location. One day, I found myself standing on a hilltop looking down into Gaza, knowing that their snipers could see me. It was a scary time, and I knew that what I was doing carried risks. But at the same time, I had no fear because I was doing what I had to do to expose the missile campaign that was terrorizing an entire population. Yes, I was committed to helping victims of terrorism. But if I had any power at all to help *stop* that terrorism, wasn't that my responsibility as well?

All together, we ended up with about 200 strong photos documenting Hamas' constant assault on southern Israel. From that group, we chose the strongest few to email to leadership in the States. The photos I took did not stop terrorism, of course; I only wish they could have. But I did what I could, and I did what was right — which is all any of us can ever ask of ourselves or each other.

. . .

One Heart Global continued to offer Survivors' Circles on a monthly basis. I always attended every month I was in town,. Each time, it was difficult to hear the stories and to see the pain — it always would be. But it was also stunning to witness the opening of so many hearts, to see the tears of sadness and relief, to watch the people who were allowing a bit of light in for the very first time. Sometimes I shared my own story, a little bit more of the poison leaving each time. Sometimes we all cried together, sometimes we laughed.

The Survivors' Circles were fluid, always changing. People came to meetings as they felt the need. We would be hosted in an individual's home, or meet in an office building or in a private room in a restaurant or bar. Barbara led many of the groups, but when she wasn't available, another psychologist or social worker would join us. We never had a set time limit; we just stayed together for a few hours until we were finished. Sometimes the groups were mostly young people, sometimes they included the elderly. The only thing that mattered is that our hearts were always there for each other.

Although One Heart Global began the Survivors' Circles by working with victims of 9/11 and victims from Israel, we always welcomed people who had experienced terrorism anywhere in the world at any time in their lives. The program grew as more people heard about the Survivors' Circles through friends or the media, and as we reached out to a variety of other organizations.

One of our participants was an Indian woman who had survived terrorism not once, but twice. She had survived both World Trade Center bombings, 1993 and 2001. She shared with us that in 1993, she was inside the building at the time of the bombing. She and others were stuck in an elevator and eventually rescued. That in itself was a terrifying experience, but then to also be involved in the 9/11 attacks was almost unimaginable.

"How could this be happening to me again? How?" she asked. "I think about that question over and over. And I still ask it today. How? I will never understand."

None of us could ever answer that question, of course.

But we could join her in asking it and support her as she openly struggled with it. I felt so honored that she joined our group and could be comfortable sharing her story, her nightmares, her fears of simply walking into a building, which the rest of us take for granted every single day. Even in this group of survivors, we could barely imagine what this woman had suffered through. We felt anguished for her pain, but she inspired all of us.

Another participant in the group was a filmmaker who was in Israel in 2003 making a documentary about a bar called Mike's Place in Tel Aviv. He chose that location because Jews, Arabs, Christians, Muslims, Israelis, Americans, and Europeans all had a good time there, and English was the "official" language. He was neither Jewish nor Muslim. His purpose was to show that people can get along regardless of their nationality or politics and, in fact, that they *do* get along every single night at Mike's Place. But on April 30 of that year, the bar was attacked by a suicide bomber while the cameras rolled. Although the filmmaker was too injured to continue filming at that moment, someone else picked up the camera and finished the story — a very different film than they had planned to make. Hearing this man speak about his experience took me right back to the Sheffield Club. I heard him, and I knew.

We were joined by an Australian man who had lost his sister in the Bali nightclub bombing in 2002. By a young Israeli woman who had been burned over 40 percent of her body in an attack. By an elderly woman and her husband who told us at the beginning that his wife wouldn't be speaking that night. He said she never spoke about what had happened to them, and he wondered if that would be all right.

"Of course. You never have to worry about that here," Barbara assured them both. "Just come sit with us."

The couple seemed comforted by that answer and they joined us in the circle. Slowly, people started to share their stories. The stories were difficult to hear that night, as they always were, and few people could make it through the telling without tears, including me. When the person seated next to the elderly woman finished her story, the husband started to say something. But the wife put her hand gently on his arm and she began to speak.

She said they were a Jewish couple with family in Israel, including a grandson whose bar mitzvah they had travelled to attend. While driving through town one day, terrorists attacked their car, and the elderly couple were both injured by gunfire. Our hearts were so full as we watched them hold each other and cry. I looked at this couple and tried to imagine the scene. How could someone hurt older people like this? I felt so much pain for them.

"It's the first time," the husband said later as he wiped his eyes. "The first time. She never . . . "

We knew what this meant to him, to her. Every single person in that room had told their story for the first time, too. We understood.

In addition to the Survivors' Circles, One Heart Global began to offer other activities. An Israeli karate instructor donated classes for survivors, to help them gain physical confidence as well as mental focus. Sometimes we met as a group just for a social activity, to lend a greater sense of normalcy to the relationships we were building. We went to restaurants, to bars, to parks, and on a boat trip around Manhattan. But wherever we went together, we always felt the emotional safety net we had created. No one had to worry or to feel "different" in this group.

I also met with people one-on-one or in groups of three

or four if they wanted. I wasn't a trained counselor or therapist, and I didn't pretend to be. I had two business degrees and looked very "together" on the outside. But I knew what it meant to be living inside a dark pit that no one else saw, what it meant to wake up exhausted from the trauma of nightmares that never seemed to end, and how frightening it could sometimes be to do the simplest thing with a group of people who had no idea what you had been through. I didn't need psychology books to tell me what life was like for these victims. I had learned first-hand how to understand others and how to help them. I also learned how to help people just from listening to their stories and understanding their pain. I learned I could help them feel safe talking and show them they can each reach a better place. I was there for one purpose: to help them survive their trauma.

We would meet sometimes for a coffee or a meal, always very informal. And although we would begin by talking about our experiences with terrorism, we would often end up by talking about the weather, politics, relationships, or the latest movie we had seen. I wanted the survivors to know that I was a safe person with whom they could discuss their nightmares and their fears. But I also wanted them to know we didn't have to always stay on the topic of grief.

I didn't meet with people to give advice or to tell them how to solve their problems. I met with survivors just to share this moment of life, to *be* with them, to show them by example that they, too, would feel a new sunrise one day. It was important for me to help them find their courage, their strength, to heal and become stronger. Maybe they weren't there yet. Maybe their darkness had to last a while longer, maybe that was part of their process, their own journey. But here I was — a healthy, strong, productive guy — promising them, modeling for them, that healing could come. That healing *would* come.

So many people in this world are in need. I remembered the man I had met with my mother at the Terror Victims' Association, the man who had not lost anyone in a terrorist attack, but whose life had been completely derailed from the emotional trauma of witnessing such a heinous act. For this man and so many others, along with their families and friends, there is such a need for understanding, empathy, and patience.

So many times I shared my story, speaking about the dark, dark days when I had wandered through my own life so painfully lost, so helpless, so hopeless, seeing nothing but suffering on my horizon. And each time, I felt a sense of gratitude of staggering proportions for the healing that had occurred in my own life, and for my ability to play some small role in bringing that healing to others. It felt like a miracle to me.

. . .

It was partly out of a sense of this gratitude, as well as a desire to know more about myself and my roots, that I started to attend synagogue and Torah class in New York.

I had been a person who really never went to synagogue unless it was a holiday or some occasion to attend with my family. But after my father's murder, my dream of his funeral, and having him visit me during the shiva and on the ship, I began to believe that something spiritual definitely existed in this world. I started going to synagogue more frequently in the initial years after his death. I certainly didn't go often or regularly, but I attended more than I had previously. And each time I went to services, I felt something so special, so powerful, like a spirit right there with me, almost sitting right beside me. It became such an emotional experience for me.

Every time the cantor would begin to chant, I would close my eyes and be so aware of God's presence with us. I was absolutely shocked how strong that feeling was for me. It was not something I had expected.

In New York, a friend introduced me to Steve Eisenberg. I knew from the moment I met Steve that he was a very special person, radiating love and kindness to everyone around him. When he looked at you and spoke to you, you felt something powerful. He had a very special aura around him that made me feel I could trust him completely and I wanted to get to know him better. Although he wasn't a rabbi, Steve led weekly Torah classes at an organization called the Jewish International Connection of New York. After attending just one class at a friend's invitation, I was hooked. I would never miss his Torah class, no matter what I had to do, no matter how busy I was or how tired I felt. If I was in New York, I was at that class. Steve's energy was so positive and his passion for Judaism was so strong, it was almost contagious.

Steve's Torah classes brought us back to the ancient texts and deeper into our current lives. He showed us that Torah could be our guidepost in every aspect of life with its wisdom and connection to God. I loved it so much that I also began attending a Torah class on Wednesdays, taught by a rabbi who also was loving and kind and concerned, and always smiling. I felt so grateful to have this opportunity to learn from both of these wise, wise men — to learn about my own roots, about my people, and about God. It's a connection to a religious and spiritual way of looking at the world that I know will always be a part of my life going forward, no matter where I live, no matter what I do.

Between this strong connection to the Jewish community, my friendship with Barbara, the relationships I was forging through One Heart Global, and my plans to expand our services, I was building a good life for myself in New York. And yet, I missed my family so badly that some days I couldn't imagine being away for even another week. I spoke to my mother all the time, of course, and I loved those conversations. I told her about my work on behalf of survivors, and she — who had continued her work with the Terror Victims' Association in Israel — told me about hers. We talked about our lives, the family, our friends. But it was never enough. It could never be as good as a hug, as good as sharing a relaxing coffee together.

I did go home fairly often during those first years in New York, even after I received my master's degree. On my first few visits home, although the family was glad to see me, they still really didn't understand what I was doing. But over time, there was a lot of publicity about One Heart Global whenever I came to Israel. My mother's friends would call her to say they had seen me on one of the morning TV shows or had read about me in the newspaper. Cousins would call, and my friends, too. The more my family and friends understood about my work, the more supportive they became.

I truly loved my work with One Heart, all the connections we were making, meeting so many people with such big hearts and willingness to do for others. But I missed my home and family so badly, there were times I felt I just couldn't stand being so far away. I thought I might have to give it all up and move back to Rishon Lezion.

One day when I was feeling particularly homesick, I called home to tell my mother I just didn't think I could stay in New York any longer.

"*Ima*, I cried on the subway this morning."

I heard the silence on the line. I didn't want my mother to worry about me, but I felt comfortable sharing with her how I was really feeling.

"Jacob, what's going on?"

"I was sitting near a little girl and boy and their voices sounded so much like Pazit's children that I could barely stand it. And when those kids got upset about something and started to cry, I started crying, too! I just miss everyone so much."

"So make another visit home as soon as you can. You know we always want to see you."

"I know. But still, it's not the same. I don't think I can do this anymore, *Ima*. I really don't." I could feel the tears in my eyes just talking about this. "I need to be with you and the family. I think it's time for me to come back home."

I could hear her take a deep breath.

"Jacob, listen to me. Look at where you are — look at the difference you are making in so many lives. I'm so proud of you. You have something so special to give people. And you were right, you could never have accomplished this in Israel. And now you want to give all that up and move back home?"

I was truly happy to hear those words from my mother.

"Jacob," she said softly. "You're crazy."

She knew that would make me laugh. And it did.

CHAPTER TWELVE

Lifting Up Teens of Terrorism

One Heart Global had been offering the Survivors' Circles for about two years when we received an email from a professor of psychology at New York University who was familiar with our work. She had learned that an organization called Tuesday's Children was offering a summer camp for teens affected by 9/11 and other terrorist attacks. She wondered if Israeli children were involved in the project. We didn't know, but we immediately contacted Tuesday's Children.

We already had discussed the idea of summer camps for teen victims of terrorism. It seemed the perfect way for teens to come together in a non-threatening, creative environment to heal and make new friends with others who truly understood what they had been through. When we heard about Tuesday's Children and discovered its mission to be similar to our own, we were very excited and worked for several months to explore a potential partnership. Eventually, we heard they would be interested in partnering for camp the following summer at a facility in Bryn Mawr, Pennsylvania. We committed to bring a group of young Israelis and to coordinate with terror victims' groups in other countries to invite their children as well.

While others stayed in New York to raise the necessary funds, work on logistics, and continue work with our Survivors' Circles, I was at home in Israel working to identify children who would be appropriate for the camp. It wasn't easy. The children needed to be ages 13 to 18, physically healthy enough to travel, and emotionally strong enough to be separated by such a long distance from their families for more than a week. I also wanted to make sure this would be their first summer camp experience; if they had previously attended a more traditional summer camp, they might be expecting something very different than what we would offer. I was eventually able to identify candidates by networking with the Terror Victims' Association and by word of mouth in the community. Once I had identified the children, I met with them and their parents to determine if the summer camp would be a good fit.

The children's stories were horrifying.

One girl had been with her family attending a cousin's bar mitzvah. The family had just stepped outside the synagogue when a suicide bomber — disguised as an Orthodox Jew — blew himself to pieces and murdered 15 people, including seven from this one family. Seven! It frightened me to even imagine the intensity of her pain. This 15-year-old became one of our first campers.

One set of teen brothers were young children when their family was attacked. The parents were shopping in a toy store when the terrorist ran in and sprayed bullets from an automatic rifle. The mother, who had been carrying the youngest child in her arms, was hit in the back as she bent over the child to shield him and was severely wounded. The father was murdered. The older boy, waiting at school for hours for his parents to pick him up, remembers an uncle driving up eventually and telling him the news that would change his life forever. I met with the boys, now 13 and 17, and their mother to talk about camp.

"It's so nice to meet you both," I told them as I held out my hand to shake theirs. The younger brother was so shy and tense, he barely looked up at me.

"You know this is not any kind of formal interview, right?" I asked them. "I promise you do not need to be afraid or worried. You know I understand what you've been through. My *abba* was taken from me, too. I know how badly that hurts." I shared my own story with them. Still, the boys were very, very quiet.

It took a while for them to warm up, but they eventually told me a little bit about themselves and their lives. I felt the camp would be so helpful for them, but I was concerned the younger one might not be ready.

"Tell me something," I said, leaning in close to the boys. "How you would feel about being far away from your *ima* for a whole week? I'll be there with you the entire time, but how will you feel leaving your *ima* at home?"

The boys didn't answer. The mother said, "They will be fine."

I had my reservations but I knew how much the summer camp could help them. In the end, we decided to take these two brothers along with three other Israelis that first summer.

In addition to the Israeli children and Tuesday's Children's 9/11 survivors, we also worked over the next two summers with organizations in England, France, Liberia, Northern Ireland, and Spain. Each organization brought several teens to the summer camp, along with a psychologist and translator.

Each of these children had suffered so much in their young lives. When they first arrived, you could just see the pain written all over their faces. Each group of teens stayed to themselves, huddled together, hardly making eye contact with anyone else. After all, everyone else was a stranger, and every stranger was suspicious. Fear kept these teens always "on alert" and kept them from speaking to anyone they did not know.

On the first day each year, I'm not sure any camper believed that any other teen in that room had been through an experience similar to their own or could truly understand their pain. In fact, we found out later that the Irish students had never heard of the conflict in the Middle East. They didn't know that Israeli teens live with terror and fear as part of their everyday reality. Many of the Israeli teens had no idea that terrorism existed in places like Northern Ireland or Spain.

We did icebreaker activities that first day, we ate together, and we talked. But at the end of the day, I was still looking at a group of teenagers whose closed faces and downcast eyes told me they wondered what in the world they were doing at this camp with a bunch of strangers whose language they couldn't even understand.

The fear and suspicion lifted very slowly. Little by little as we spent time together — working on art projects, playing music and sports, eating and talking, participating in therapy sessions, sharing classes in leadership and conflict resolution, laughing and crying together — the teens began to see each other as individuals not so dissimilar from their own friends and families back home. By the fourth day each summer, the translators were working constantly, running from place to place as teens from all nations talked and laughed together and mixed into one great group. Every minute, someone took another group selfie.

No wonder it took these children time to trust each other. We heard such heartbreaking stories. One camper from Northern Ireland survived the blast of a pipe bomb when he was just 4 years old. Another Northern Ireland teen lost a grandfather, an aunt, three uncles, and three cousins — a total of eight people in three generations of one family murdered in terrorist attacks!

Two campers from France had been in Cairo on a school trip. As they had walked together with a third friend in a market area, a terrorist bomb exploded, killing the friend, who had been standing right next to them. One camper from Spain lost his mother in the terrorist attacks on the commuter trains in Madrid. One young man lost his sister in the nightclub bombings in Bali, Indonesia. So many campers from New York had lost parents in the 9/11 attacks.

The list of suffering went on and on.

It was not easy to hear these stories — not for me or for any of the campers. We watched these teenagers break down in tears as they told their stories to this unique group, unafraid to share details they had kept inside for years, sharing fears and pain they didn't feel able to share with friends, or even family.

Only on a rare occasion did we have a camper who never completely opened up to the group. Samuel, one such teen, was originally from Liberia and now lived on Staten Island with his grandmother and brother. He was so lovely, so polite and kind, warm and easygoing, and he made friends with everyone right away. But the way Samuel shared his story let us know that he wasn't ready to completely open up. Samuel's family lived through the terror of the second Liberian Civil War. He told us only that he had lost his father, and he made it clear that was the end of his story. We never knew any more than that.

Samuel and I have stayed friends to this day, and I have

had the pleasure of visiting his home and meeting his entire family and his girlfriend. Whenever I ask him how he's doing, he still answers, "I'm fine!" But after getting to know him over a period of years, I have come to recognize the subtle clues in his voice that tell me how he's really doing. At summer camp, he never did share his darkest memories and fears, and he has never shared them with me individually. Even so, at least he's learned he's not alone.

The violence described by our campers had been in the news for a few days in their home countries, some even internationally. Flags were lowered, funerals were held, politicians came on television to decry the evil, memorials were built. And all of that was important, very important.

But what happens next? What happens to these traumatized children when the community's attention has moved on, when the world's attention has moved to the next financial crisis or political campaign or even to the next terrorist attack? What happens to these terror victims the next month or the next year — when the teen who still has shrapnel in his leg has to walk into gym class? Or two years later, when the senior in high school can't explain or even understand why she has no motivation to go to college? Or 10 years later, when the young adult can't seem to hold a job, always angry at anyone telling him what to do, even a supervisor or boss? Or 20 years later, when the married father of two beautiful children finds himself drinking every single night just to dull the pain and fear he still cannot understand?

In Hebrew, we have only one word to describe someone who has been impacted by a terrorist attack. But that one word is translated into English as both "survivor" and "victim." Is someone a victim if he is murdered at an attack? Or course. Is someone a survivor if she lives through the attack? Of course. But the person who lives through a terror attack or loses a loved one to terrorism or witnesses thousands of lives being taken at once, even if she knew none of them personally — *all those survivors are also victims.* And victims of any crime need support and help. While the world's attention inevitably moves on to something new, these victims are still suffering and these victims still need and deserve support.

Physical injuries have a beginning, a middle, and an end — even those as severe and complex as my father's injuries from his car accident. There is a path, a plan against which to measure progress, alternate plans to turn to when necessary. Many physical injuries can heal completely. If you're lucky, they can even heal to such an extent that you can absolutely forget about them. It is possible to go back to being essentially the same as your former self.

But trauma stays with you for a lifetime. It never allows you to go back to being your former self. You can never again be innocent and absolutely sure that tomorrow will bring the same security and love that today brought. You can never go back to being *that* person. But with the appropriate support, victims of trauma *can* move forward into wonderful, full lives.

I was so blessed to receive free support provided by the State of Israel after my father's murder. That psychological care was life-changing for me and helped me grow into the man I am today. But what if I need care in the future? Post-Traumatic Stress Disorder — which I had been suffering from, although we didn't use the term in Israel in 2002 — does not evaporate. Nightmares never completely end. Worry and fear and anxiety could still plague me. Like any trauma survivor, I could need help in the future. Even in Israel, a country that faces terrorism on a continual basis, there is no program to provide that long-term support. Israel does provide psychologists immediately after an attack. But the time period for accessing that help is limited, while the time period for suffering and needing that help is not.

At One Heart Global, we continually worked toward offering that unlimited support. We worked to develop groups of psychologists who were willing to donate their services to terror victims whenever it would be needed, whether now or years from now. We worked to develop lists of organizations internationally that could help victims at any time. And we worked with medical doctors and hospitals that were willing to donate their services and materials to provide plastic surgery for terror victims, no matter when the victim decided it was time.

It is a start. Much more work needs to be done to support these innocents as they move forward to build healthy, strong lives. And they *can* build those lives by getting the help they need, by living in a process of healing.

. . .

The first two years of our summer camps took place in conjunction with Tuesday's Children. But beginning the third year, One Heart moved the summer camps to New York City and led them on our own, renaming the camps our "Young Ambassadors" program. Just as in the previous years, we raised the money to bring children from Israel, whom I personally met in advance. We also connected with international terror victims' support groups who brought teens from their own countries. In New York, we sometimes housed the group at a hotel that donated the space. Or, if we didn't have donated space that particular year, we asked the Jewish community to open their homes to the students and group leaders.

We did many of the same activities at our Young Ambassadors program that we had offered at the Bryn Mawr summer camps. But being in New York gave us some additional opportunities.

First, in addition to general New York City sightseeing, museums, and entertainment, we were able to introduce the teens to local and national leaders. I remembered my own trip to the States with OneFamily and how much it meant when a person of stature took time to meet with me, to look me in the eye, to offer me support in a hug or to say — by his or her very presence with me — that I was important. Without a doubt, I had become stronger by being with Giuliani, Bloomberg, and all the community leaders we met, and I wanted our teens to have that experience, too.

Over the course of several years, we gave our Young Ambassadors the opportunity to meet with leaders including U.N. Ambassador from Israel Meron Reuben, U.N. Ambassador from Ireland Anne Anderson, Israel Consul General Asaf Shariv, New York City Police Commissioner Ray Kelly, and several senators and congressmen.

One of the most impressive figures these Young Ambassadors met was New York Gov. David Paterson, and we were so honored that he gave us his time. Gov. Paterson is legally blind because of an illness that struck him in infancy, but he never let that "disability" stop him from accomplishing more than most sighted people. He gave our Young Ambassadors so much by talking to them, listening to some of their own stories of great difficulty, and encouraging them in every way he could. I remember the looks on their faces as they listened to him, so impressed and motivated by his words, understanding perhaps for the first time that a person with a "problem" can become an inspirational leader to others. It was a meeting I'm sure they will never forget.

The second way our teens benefited from our New York

location was the opportunity to visit Ground Zero on a tour led by Lee Ielpi, a firefighter whose firefighter son was murdered in the 9/11 attacks. This was a very moving and painful visit for our teens, some of whom had lost their own loved ones on 9/11. But whether or not they had a personal connection to this particular attack, our teens knew that Mr. Ielpi *knew* their pain. He spoke to them as a community leader who had been instrumental in the rescue operation at Ground Zero — including recovering the remains of his own son — and who has dedicated the rest of his life to educating people about 9/11.

Standing strong and tall in the community, Mr. Ielpi served as another model, another example of a victim who was moving forward and serving others. No one thought for a minute that Mr. Ielpi's pain was over. We all knew he missed his son with a deep and abiding pain every single day, just as our Young Ambassadors missed their own loved ones. But he showed them that it was possible to move forward nevertheless.

Probably the toughest day for our campers and Young Ambassadors each year was the final day. After being together for a week, these teens had developed very deep friendships in the largest group they'd ever experienced of people who really knew what they had been through. They had shared their life stories, exchanged photos and T-shirts, even traded eyeglasses, everything they could do to intertwine their lives together. It was so difficult for them to say good-bye. They were not only crying, they were absolutely sobbing. Fully grown teens, some of them taller than me and the other staff members, just crying their hearts out.

These victims of terrorism who had come together so closed and suspicious had gradually opened up to feel the security and love One Heart offered. In this place, in this group, they could relax. No one was going to tell them that their father's murder was 10 years ago and so they should be "over" it. No one would force them into speaking if they needed a time of silence. But if they did want to speak, this group listened and accepted every word said with open hearts. And now they did not want to leave to go back to communities that might not understand them as deeply — or worse, to communities where terrorism was still a daily threat. Those goodbye hugs were some of the most emotional moments of my life. We hugged and hugged, but eventually, it was time to leave. And I have to admit that I cried like a baby, too — although, like my mother, I prefer my tears to be private.

During several of the camps, our campers did a project that involved giving back to the community. In conjunction with Tuesday's Children, we had the students clean up a city field that was in bad shape, or meet and correspond with children who had cancer. We included these "mitzvah projects" in our curriculum for two reasons. First, these projects were a way for the students to "pay forward" the benefits they received from camp. Second, and even more importantly, although our campers had been the ones to need help for so long, these projects let them know they had the strength to be givers, as well as receivers.

We all have the responsibility to do what we can to make things better in our world. But some people are so injured, so traumatized that they no longer believe they have any ability or value to offer anyone else. We wanted our campers to experience the fact that they did have the ability, the power and character to make a difference, whether in the life of a community or an individual.

One day not long after our campers had written letters to local children with cancer, one of the psychologists came running up to me, screaming my name as I was walking with a group of campers.

"I need to talk to you," she said. But it was clear that she didn't want to say anything in front of the campers. So I suggested we go for a walk. The psychologist told me one of our teens, a boy named David, had written a very disturbing letter.

"He told the child not to worry about death. He said death isn't scary, and it's OK to die," the psychologist said. "Jacob, I'm afraid he's suicidal. I'm very worried he might try to kill himself."

I was terrified and heartbroken to think about the pain this teen must be in. We conferred with the psychologists on staff, who didn't want to confront him and send him to a hospital, not believing that was best for his healing process. However, we made sure David was supervised every minute for the rest of the camp. If he was walking to an activity, we made sure he had a buddy walk with him. If he was going back to his room for the night, we made sure someone was with him. The psychologist from his own group spent as much time talking with him as possible, and we contacted the appropriate psychologists back in his hometown to make sure he would have the continuing care he needed when he returned home.

I also took it on myself to spend more time with David, being with him every day to talk, to share stories, to listen. I learned that he had very few friends at home. He felt so alone and unable to imagine a life for himself beyond his pain and rejection. I certainly knew how that felt. We talked a lot about what it meant to be responsible for your own life, what it meant to have strength, how it was possible to be happy carrying around the pain we both felt in our hearts. We spoke about the family members we lost, what kind of people they were, how much we missed them. My heart just absolutely went out to this teenager who was suffering so badly, and we developed an important relationship.

I stayed in contact with him when camp was over. We emailed back and forth quite a bit and occasionally spoke on the phone. I wanted to make sure he knew he could count on me. I wasn't going to turn my back on him, no matter what his friends did. I didn't judge him. I was there for him, and he could rely on that.

The following year, when David came back to camp, he was an absolute superstar. He was in such good shape emotionally and physically, you could just see his strength. He participated in everything, enjoyed everything, and helped the other campers every chance he had. Even the camp leaders turned to him when they needed some help with an activity. It was just a wonder to see him. We were so proud of him, and we made sure he knew it.

How did this happen? How did this struggling, rejected, depressed teenager become such a powerful young man?

I believe David's transformation, and that of so many of our campers, came about because he wanted this change and because he was in a place where he could get the help he needed, where others were willing to share their strength with him.

When you are strong in your heart, your motives are selfless and pure, you truly listen to others' stories and are absolutely present with them. And when you let them know that *you* see them as a valuable human being, then you have the ability to share your strength with someone who needs it.

I believe this because I've seen it over and over. This is how Esther helped me at such a critical time in my own life. No matter how despondent and lost I felt, she consistently reflected back to me my value as a human being. She respected where I was in my life and respected the feelings I shared with her, but she also made it clear that she saw something more in me, something I thought I had lost — my power.

By the time I started seeing Esther, I wanted to change. I wanted to stop feeling so much pain every day, and I was willing to ask for the help I needed. I will give myself credit for that — because you do have to *want* to change, in order to bring about a change in your life. But then, once my heart was open and I asked for help? Then God blessed me by bringing Esther into my life, a professional who dedicated her whole life to helping others, to helping them find their own lost selves. Esther modeled for me how to be fully present with people, how to love and honor them, and how to listen with your heart. I do not have Esther's professional training, but I will always carry her example with me.

I carry my father's example as well. What a wonderful listener he was! My father was always truly present with people, and they recognized his pure heart. This is why the patients at the many clinics he went to after his accident told him their stories, why they considered him to be a friend, and how he helped them even when they could hardly envision their own future. I remember one particular man who lost his leg, similar to my father. This man couldn't handle the change in his life, the phantom limb pain, the fact he wasn't able to walk on two legs, couldn't run, and couldn't be the person he used to be. My father would meet with him to encourage him to continue his life, to dig deep to find his strength. Even during his own painful recovery, my father encouraged this man in every way he could.

No one has ever set a better example of what it means to be a survivor than my father. One day he sets off to work, a regular man with a wife and three children. And the next he is near death with only one leg and hands that are barely held together with pins and thread. What did my father do in response? He became the strongest man I have ever known. My father showed me that our lives can change in an instant, taking us from our familiar self to someone we barely recognize. He showed me that with hard work and belief, we can rebuild our strength in our soul and create a better reality around us — even if it will never be as it was before.

There is hope and courage in each one of us, and it's up to us to find it. My father taught me that we can make it through anything. And that's what I worked to pass on to David and every other survivor.

CHAPTER THIRTEEN
My New Sunrise

During the years I worked with the Survivors' Circles and the summer camps, constantly going back and forth between Israel and the States, I was also enjoying my social life. My circle of friends in New York was growing every month, my connections in the Jewish community were deepening with my twice-weekly Torah studies, and I was dating here and there, although I hadn't found the long-term special connection I was looking for.

Then I met a young woman named Alecia.

Alecia and I met through the Jewish online dating service JDate, so we knew immediately that we shared certain values and were both looking for a Jewish partner. I learned online that Alecia was a well-educated and well-traveled public-relations professional. She was a gorgeous young woman. We chatted for a while online to get to know each other, spoke by phone, and then agreed we wanted to meet in person.

Our first date was at a Mexican restaurant in the city. I don't remember whether the restaurant was very busy that night, but I hope for their sake they weren't — because we sat talking for hours and hours. We started off chatting about life in general, New York City, and how difficult the singles dating scene could be. She talked about her sister and parents. I spoke about my mother and family back in Israel. Then she asked me to share more about myself and the work I do.

While I spoke about my father's murder and the One Heart work that brought me to New York, I watched her face very closely. Most people are polite enough to listen when they've asked you to speak about yourself, but I felt something else, something deeper, happening with Alecia.

She told me how genuinely sorry she was for my loss. Then she said, "I guess I've been impacted by a terrorist attack, too."

"You guess?"

"I was downtown on 9/11," she said. "But I just never thought about myself as a victim or a survivor because I didn't lose anyone."

She told me she had moved to New York City on September 6, 2001 to take a job, a 22-year-old fresh out of college. Her offices were scheduled to move into the World Trade Center, but had been delayed until mid-September. So she was in a temporary space downtown, a few blocks away. She loved her newfound freedom, her new apartment, the excitement of working in the city. But five days later, life was turned upside down. Alecia came up out of the subway just minutes after the first plane hit the Tower, and was standing just a few blocks away when the second plane struck. Not knowing how to get home, she went to her temporary offices and with her colleagues, sat in fear for their lives until finally evacuating after the second tower had fallen.

At one point, Alecia was able to get through to her father's cell. She let him know she was OK, and told him that she loved him — and to make sure to tell her mom and sister as well. He told her to be calm, that everything would be all right.

Not knowing if her daughter was safe, her mother in Texas watched the horrifying images on television — along with my family in Israel and the rest of the world. All of us were terrorized by the events of that day.

Afterwards, for many, it was over. And after that, it was long over. But not for Alecia.

As we spoke in the restaurant that night, Alecia shared with me some of the feelings she had experienced, the images, the fears, the nightmares. What I didn't know until later was that she had never spoken about 9/11 in such detail before, not in all the intervening years. It was difficult for her family and friends to understand that Alecia had suffered a trauma that day at all. And since she had never viewed herself as a victim, she thought it was wrong to seek help. She felt guilty about her feelings as she hadn't lost anyone personally, while others had lost so much.

But I understood. I knew she would always remember the sounds she heard that day, the rumblings, the vibrations of the buildings as they fell, bringing thousands to their deaths in an instant. I understood she would always remember the smells of that day, the feeling of the dust in her nose, on her clothes. I understood.

From that very first dinner, Alecia and I knew there was something special between us. A first date is usually a time to speak about fun things, often meaningless conversation, just a way to be with the other person and to see how you feel together. But here we were — two strangers just hours earlier, now sharing some of the most important aspects of our lives, completely honestly, connected in a very special and deep way. We both felt it. I recognized that Alecia was very much like my mother, the highest compliment I could pay anyone — a very strong, sensitive, and kind woman.

It was a truly magical time for us, Israeli and American, both victims of terror, both people who love life and want to live it the best possible way. We planned our second date right after the first one and, again, we lost track of time, spending hours talking in Times Square, walking with our coffees in our hands, looking at each other's eyes and knowing this is only the beginning of something very special. The next time we met, we didn't care what we did as long as we were together. We walked in Union Square and decided to catch a movie. What movie? I don't remember now, and we didn't care then. We just wanted to be close to each other. I couldn't stop staring at Alecia's beautiful eyes.

Now as husband and wife, Alecia and I are so grateful for our unique bond. Whenever she speaks about 9/11 and shares her story with others, I can see her become stronger and stronger. I always try to catch her eye just to let her know how proud I am of her courage. And whenever I cry in a movie about a beautiful relationship between a man and his father — and I do — she understands exactly where those emotions come from. I don't have to hold in my tears or pretend those feelings aren't there. We support each other on every level, and I am so blessed.

. . .

While I learned so much from our campers and Young Ambassadors during those summers, I also learned from the psychologists and group leaders who accompanied them. Most importantly, I learned that Europe had a vibrant and extensive network of professional organizations advocating on behalf of terrorism victims. Neither Israel nor the U.S. had a meaningful representation in those networks. The Europeans were far ahead of us in highlighting the needs of these victims, led most impressively by the work of the European Network of Associations of Victims of Terrorism and the Spanish organization, Associación Victimas Del Terrorismo. Through my relationship with the Spanish AVDT, One Heart Global became one of the major U.S. partner organizations to join the International Congress for Victims of Terrorism.

In 2009, I participated in my first Congress, held in Madrid that year, as the only Israeli invited to attend and one of the very few representatives from U.S. organizations. I was excited about all I wanted to share with the European leaders, the local victims, the heads of participating organizations, and the media — but also very nervous. I worked on my speech for days, knew it by heart before I stepped on that stage, and fielded a question-and-answer session. I felt comfortable with my presentation and did my best to respond to all the questions carefully and thoughtfully.

And then an Irish gentleman came forward to ask, "Mr. Kimchy, are you really so sure Hamas is a terrorist organization?" he asked. "They provide so many important services for the people of the Middle East. In fact, we held a fundraiser for Hamas right in our own community."

It took me a few seconds to catch my breath. How was it possible that Hamas, which has murdered hundreds and hundreds of civilians in Israel, is not known in Europe as a terrorist organization? I took the time I needed to gather my thoughts and I provided the most thorough answer I could, to make sure this man would never again doubt that the people who killed my father and so many others do indeed belong to a cruel terrorist organization.

The following year, I was one of 600 invited to attend the Congress, again held in Spain. It was an extraordinary opportunity to again be with the victims and organizations from all over the world, some of whom I had worked with the previous year. As one of only 20 people invited to speak, I recognized it as a huge responsibility. Again the only Israeli in attendance at the Congress, I participated in a panel with victims and representatives from France, Italy, the U.S., Colombia, and Ireland. I spoke that day in memory of my father and to honor all those who are no longer able to raise their voices.

"Terrorism will never win. We are all together, stronger and united, with a smile next to our pain," I said. "No one will break our spirit, and forever we will remember our loved ones."

The Congress was very widely publicized all over Europe. It was so heartening to know these issues were being taken seriously and brought to the attention of the wider population via a level of media exposure I had never seen in the States or in Israel. But I didn't truly understand the respect Europeans have for victims of terrorism until the 600 of us were taken on buses to a "special event." We were told only that the event would be a celebration held in our honor in the town of Salamanca.

The buses brought us to the exterior of one of the town's most famous plazas. We were walked down a white carpet through a shaded narrow walkway into the bright sunlight of the plaza's large interior. We heard some background music coming from the inside of the plaza, but we had no idea what we were about to experience. And then we saw it — a crowd of 10,000 people cheering for us, supporting us, lending us their strength! It was absolutely overwhelming to feel such a level of love and support from so many, many strangers. I took out my camera and filmed this once-in-a-lifetime moment to be able to show my family and friends how remarkable the Spanish people are. I looked around me at my friends — victims from all over the world — all amazed, and all with tears in our eyes.

Not long afterward, we were told a few of us would be honored at an outdoor reception to include a visit from the royal family, represented by Prince Felipe and Princess Letizia, now King Felipe VI and Queen Letizia of Spain.

"Jacob, you will be the one to welcome the prince and princess," the event organizer said to me.

"I'm absolutely honored," I said. "But who will welcome them with me? And what is the protocol for welcoming a prince and princess?"

The organizer looked at me and smiled. "You'll welcome them by yourself outside the hall. They'll arrive in 20 minutes. Regarding the protocol, I really have no idea. Wait here and I'll try to find out." At that, she left me standing alone. Alone and nervous. She came back to get me just before the prince and princess were to make their entrance to say that several other terror victims would be joining me to welcome the royal couple. She said we should feel comfortable to say whatever we want.

"Remember, the prince and princess are here to support all of you, so say whatever you'd like. But if you want to be formal, just say something like, 'Nice to meet you your highness,' and maybe put your head down a little bit." I had no idea if that was the appropriate protocol, and I still don't. But I did what she said, and everything seemed to be all right.

The royal couple could not have been more kind and genuinely concerned with the issues of terrorism and victims' needs. They walked into the yard surrounded with guards, shook our hands, thanked each of us for coming, and gave each of us a chance to share whatever we wanted to say with them. After that, we gathered with the royal family, the head of parliament, and the head of the courts to take a group photo. As I stood there, as strong and proud as I could be with the leadership of Spain, I asked my father to be with me at that moment.

Later, we answered questions from reporters, all of whom seemed so genuinely interested in the issues, and I had the privilege to speak in a very small group with a few parliament members and the prince and princess, all surrounded by security. I told them about my father, his murder by the Hamas suicide bomber, and the fact that nothing was left of my father's body. I remember the Prince looking and me, saying he was so sorry.

"I am in shock," the prince said. "There was nothing left for you to bury?"

"Nothing," I answered. As we continued to speak, I described the situation of terrorism in Israel, the pain of the many victims of 9/11 I met in NYC, and the mission of One Heart.

The future King of Spain turned to me and thanked me for my story. "Spain has suffered terribly from terrorism, too," he said. "We should all be strong against it."

Since then, I have had the opportunity to speak out and represent victims of terrorism in so many venues. Each time, it's both an honor and a learning experience for me. I've spoken in Israel as the representative of all Rishon Lezion terror victims at an event with the mayor of our city. I've had the opportunity to speak to at-risk students, to share my strength and help them envision a way forward into a brighter future for themselves. In New York City at an event celebrating Israel Independence Day, I spoke on the U.S.S. Intrepid in front of 5,000 people — immediately after Mayor Michael Bloomberg and before Israel U.N. Representative Gabriela Shalev. In the Netherlands I spoke in front of the Minister of Law and several local organizations that help victims of terror.

I also participated in a meeting with the British Parliament during a discussion about funding for survivors of the London bombings. During the first year after the bombings, funds had been appropriated for survivor support. Now they were planning to remove those funds from the coming year's budget. I did everything I could to make them listen to my point of view.

"But no one came forward to ask for help," the minister said. "Why should we keep it in the budget if no one wants it? We have so many other real needs."

"But they're all still in shock," I explained. "They are just beginning to understand what happened to them, and they will be trauma victims for the rest of their lives. They will need help. Please let it be there for them when they're ready to come forward."

Two years ago, I was invited to speak on Israeli national TV on Yom Hazikaron, our Day of Remembrance for the Fallen Soldiers and Victims of Terrorism. Although this day is sometimes called Israel's Memorial Day, it is nothing like Memorial Day in the States.

In Israel, Yom Hazikaron is a time to honor and respect those whose voices can no longer be heard. All television channels stop regular programming to show tributes to the fallen. All schools hold only special activities to pay tribute and educate the students about their country's history. Rallies and speeches are everywhere. And in addition, at the sound of a specific siren blast, the entire country stops for a one-minute memorial of silence. Every business, factory, school, every bus and car on every road and highway in the country — everything comes to a complete stop as we collectively pay our respects to our fallen.

At the ceremony, I was seated with Prime Minister Benjamin Netanyahu, President Shimon Peres, Chief of Staff of the Israeli Defense Forces Lt-Gen. Benjamin Gantz, the Israeli ministers of security and defense, numerous other Israeli leaders and ambassadors from other countries, my mother, and a man who had lost a daughter to terrorism. At the moderator's nod, I left my seat and walked to the stage as the moderator read a short statement about me and spoke about my father. At that moment, every television channel in Israel was broadcasting this one event, with cameras focused only on me. I used every bit of energy I could find within myself to stand up and speak. Once again, I spoke in memory of Rami Kimchy.

I recited the Kaddish prayer that day, one of the biggest honors of my life. The Kaddish prayer is familiar to most Jews as the mourner's Kaddish, a prayer that is said as a part of our mourning rituals. Consequently, its words and cadence often have such a sad connotation. But the truth is that death is never mentioned in the Kaddish. At a time of mourning and loss, we come together to recite a prayer that praises God's greatness and asks that God's kingdom of peace and healing be established on earth. This theme of the Kaddish has come to play a central role in my own life.

I stood there a moment before I started to speak and took a deep breath. Although I know my father's spirit is all around me and not in any one particular place, I remember looking up at the sky right then. I also looked at my mother and saw the sadness in her eyes. I wanted to give her a big hug right then, but instead, I started to speak.

I worked so hard to get where I was right then, staying focused on the memory of my father, on my goal of helping victims. I gave every inch of my energy to make it happen — left my country, left my family and friends, and even risked my master's degree. How did this happen? Courage. Hope. As well as the fear that came from being in such a bad place.

I felt like I was climbing uphill constantly, *never* stopping, sometimes breathing so heavily I didn't know how I could continue. But just then, people would come forward with exactly the encouragement I needed — along with occasional comments that I found disturbing.

"Wow, Jacob! You travel all over the world and you meet such important people. You have such a great life! You're so lucky!"

I've heard those kinds of comments so many times over the past few years, received them in emails, seen them on my Facebook page. And each time, I want to reply, "Are you kidding?"

Lucky? If I had been lucky, I would have had my father with me when I earned my two college degrees. I would have been able to watch his eyes light up when I introduced him to Alecia. I would have had the honor of helping my father and mother as they grew old together. So no, I'm not so lucky. If I were given a choice, I would gladly give up all the travel, the speaking, the conversations with dignitaries for just one more hug in my father's arms. Everyone who carries within themselves the ache for a lost loved one knows exactly what I mean: everything in exchange for just one more hug.

But we're not given that choice, are we? Instead, I decided to take responsibility into my own hands, responsibility for my life and for as many others as I can help. We're always given the opportunity to make the most of what we do have, to learn from the experiences of others, to ask for the help we need. So I made the decision I would win and terrorism would lose; I would stand strong in front of the hand of terrorism and take with me all those who weren't able to stand up by themselves.

Whenever I speak in front of a crowd to explain what it means to be a trauma victim, I want to make sure everyone understands that the person sitting right next to them could be suffering from a deep trauma. Yes, even the person who is smiling at everyone and telling jokes, even the person wearing beautiful clothes, eating in fancy restaurants, and driving beautiful cars.

One day, one of my mother's best friends, a woman who also lost her husband to terrorism in Israel, went to the government office that provides victims' services. When this woman finally met with a social worker in the department, the social worker looked at her and said, "You lost your husband? Really? But you look so wonderful. You belong in a fashion magazine!"

My mother's friend ran out of the room crying. She couldn't believe that the person whose job it is to *help* victims could be so insensitive and hurtful. She called my mother, who helped her calm down and then drove directly over to that office. I wasn't there to witness my mother in action, but I feel sure that social worker will never be so insensitive and insulting to another terrorism victim again.

Yes, maybe my mother's friend did look physically just as she had before her husband's murder. Yes, maybe she wanted to look beautiful again, for herself, for her family, maybe even to attract a man again. It's not a crime to want to move on with our lives. But just barely beneath that surface lives a woman for whom trauma has changed *everything* — from the very way she breathes to the way she thinks, to the way she feels about every person and event in her life.

Terrorism caused the trauma in this woman's life and in mine. But the issue of trauma is much bigger than terrorism.

People can be traumatized by so many, many events, and what might not seem like a big problem for one person can be experienced as intense trauma by another. In addition to physical or emotional abuse, financial problems, a divorce, a child wandering off lost from a parent for even a few minutes, even certain academic exams — all can provoke a traumatic reaction, sometimes for many, many years. None of us wears a sticker on our forehead or specific color clothing indicating that we're coping with a trauma. You can never tell who's suffering just by looking in from the outside.

A few years ago I had an opportunity to remind someone of that exact fact. I could have let the occasion pass, but I chose not to. I was home in Israel when I saw my high-school principal at an event, and I went up to speak with her.

"Do you remember me?" I asked.

"I'm sorry?" I could see that she couldn't place me. I couldn't blame her — after all, 18 years had passed.

"It's Jacob Kimchy." I could see her start to smile. "Now do you remember me?"

"Jacob! Of course! I didn't recognize you." And this woman who had been my nemesis for so many years gave me a hug. "You look wonderful. How are you doing? What are you up to?"

"Actually, I am doing very well, thank you. I've earned my bachelor's degree and my master's degree and I've founded a non-profit organization in New York City."

"Wow. Congratulations. That's extremely impressive."

"Especially from me, right?"

"I didn't say . . ."

"I'm actually the first of my friends to have earned a master's degree. I bet you didn't expect that," I said.

"Well . . . "

"It's OK," I said. "You can say the truth. In fact, I'd like to talk about the truth. I was a horrible student in high school. I skipped school every chance I got. I was in trouble all the time. In fact, some weeks I spent more time in your office than in the classroom."

We both smiled. "Actually, that is how I remember you," she said. "I can't say I would have thought you'd be the first to have a graduate degree. You were one tough guy in high school, Kimchy."

"But did you ever wonder why?"

"Why what?"

"Why I was such a terrible student, why I never wanted anything to do with school. Did you ever wonder?"

She shook her head. "I guess I just figured you were a teenager."

"I wish you had asked me why I was always in your office, why I didn't study. I wish you'd really wanted to know." And I sat with her then, explaining about my father's accident, the teacher in fifth grade that had thrown me into the wall, the teacher who just screamed and screamed at us, all my fears as a student.

"I didn't want to be a failure. I wanted to be a good student," I told her. "I just did not know what to do with all my feelings."

My principal apologized to me, and I could tell she was sincere. And she thanked me for sharing such an important lesson, one she said she would take forward into her communication with all her students going forward.

When I decided to dedicate myself to helping others who had been traumatized — by any source, not just terrorism — it was because I knew how many of us were suffering on the inside, no matter what we look like on the outside. I'll never forget the words Moshe used to describe his feelings to me just a few days after our father's murder — his sense that he could come crashing down at any moment with my father no longer there to hold him up. I want to be the strength for those who feel no one is behind them to hold them up. And being that person for others helps me to continue healing through my own trauma, as well.

Once I made that decision to help others as well as work through my own trauma, I became exceedingly "lucky." Or, as I have come to see it, led and blessed by the hand of God.

I have no doubt that it was God who brought Esther and the support group into my life at a time when I could hardly feel anything other than pain. Was it a coincidence that I found myself seated near a psychologist who focused on grief work and trauma, among the thousands and thousands of stranded passengers crowded into the airport that day? Or that a woman whose business had donated its services on the OneFamily trip was on an airplane with me a year later and we reconnected only because I couldn't sleep? Was it a coincidence that a friend introduced me to an exceptional Torah teacher, such a wise man who helped me learn so much about faith and God? Was it a coincidence that Alecia and I found each other?

To many people, the answer is yes — all of these connections are arbitrary, random, probability-related events and nothing more. And there was a time in my life when I would have agreed with that. But not now.

Yes, it's true that life is full of sadness and suffering. But that is not the whole, complete truth. Life is also full of joy and love and the opportunity to grow and learn. Do we want to open our hearts to see that joy and those opportunities? Or do we want to develop a view that continually focuses on the negative and concludes that life is meaningless? God left us here to decide.

I have made my choice. I have decided to thank God for my existence by choosing to see a world filled with the potential for love and goodness — and to work toward making it better by bringing whatever light I can into the dark spaces. I choose to thank God for helping my father recover from his accident, for giving our family 14 more wonderful years of his love and growth, for allowing him to live to see his grandchildren.

I believe that every morning is a chance for change, for love, for growth, for each of us to become our better selves. There are so many times in life when we want to achieve something — whether a better job, a better relationship, better grades or to become emotionally or physically stronger — and the only thing stopping us is ourselves. It is up to us to decide where we want to be tomorrow. Yes, sometimes it feels like there's a deep river between where we are now and where we want to be. But we are the only one who can keep us from reaching the other side of that river. If we believe we can cross it, if we know that it's all right to ask for help and to hold others' hands as we walk together, if we know it's all right to open our hearts and share our fear, if we will take that first step, then I believe God will always be right next to us on that path.

. . .

Life in this world so often involves layers and layers of complexity. It can be difficult to even discern which questions need answering, much less to develop the best answer. That is certainly true in Israel, where you can be absolutely sure you know the correct answers to the complex questions of security, justice, and politics — until one day you realize you don't.

In June 2006, the month One Heart Global held our first Survivor's Circle, a young Israeli soldier named Gilad Shalit was captured by Hamas. Terrorists had tunneled under the border between Gaza and Israel and emerged spraying gunfire directly at Corporal Shalit's tank. Two Israeli soldiers were killed, three were wounded, and Shalit was taken hostage. The army sent troops into Gaza to locate and retrieve Shalit, but they were unsuccessful. At that point, the Israeli government said it would not negotiate with terrorists for Shalit's release.

Throughout Israel and the Jewish diaspora, rallies were held and funds were raised. Ambassadors at the U.N. called for Shalit's unconditional and immediate release. I also participated in rallies supporting Shalit and calling for his release. In fact, at one of those rallies, an individual told me he knew of a group who was willing to give millions of dollars in ransom in exchange for Shalit. I contacted an agent in Israeli Intelligence who was a friend of mine, telling him about the group and asking if he thought the government would consider it. My friend said it could be an amazing offer, but the Israeli Intelligence couldn't accept it. At that point, they did not want any third party involved.

Gilad Shalit lived in captivity for five years.

In 2011, after working through the Egyptian and German governments, Israel reached an agreement to secure Shalit's release. But the cost was high: In exchange for this one Israeli soldier, Israel would release 1,027 Palestinian prisoners from its jails during a period of several months. Among the prisoners to be released was one terrorist known to be responsible for orchestrating my father's murder, as well as several other Hamas terrorists who were thought to have been involved in the attack.

My country was releasing my father's murderers.

Judging by the television news, the world was thrilled. Gilad Shalit had become something of a folk hero during the years of his imprisonment, and people all over the world were thrilled to see him coming home. As a former soldier myself, I wanted every single Israeli soldier home on our soil, absolutely. But at what cost?

How could it be that the terrorists who planned the murder of my father and so many other innocents would be walking free? What type of "justice" was that? I was adamantly against the prisoner exchange. You do not negotiate with terrorists. You do not allow more than 1,000 prisoners — including murderers — to walk free. If that's how you run your country, what moral ground do you have to stand on? As far as I was concerned, they were bringing Shalit home in a deal made with the devil.

But it was done. On October 18, 2011, Gilad Shalit was released to Israel.

Not long afterward, I was hosting a small gathering in my New York apartment for Israel's Deputy Foreign Minister Zev Elkin when I received a text from a New York friend. The text read: "Don't tell anyone, don't say anything. But Gilad Shalit is in town, and if you want, you can go meet him at . . ." and she gave me an address. When the event ended and the Deputy Foreign Minister and the guests left, I went to the address I had been given.

The location turned out to be a bar. I walked in and I saw Shalit sitting at the bar with a few other soldiers from his unit and a few members of the community who, like me, had been invited to meet him. Although guards were present, everything was very informal. I walked up to him and sitting on his left side, I shook his hand.

"Gilad, my name is Jacob. It's so nice to meet you," I said. "I got your information from a friend who asked me to come see you."

"Hello, Jacob. Thank you for coming."

"I'm an Israeli, Gilad. I was born in Rishon Lezion." I shared some thoughts with him about New York City and told him how happy I was that he was here now.

Then I told him that my father was murdered in 2002 by Hamas.

He looked at me carefully. "I am so sorry." And he told me exactly how many Hamas terrorists had been exchanged for his release.

"You have nothing to apologize for," I told him. "I am just so happy you are here."

And I meant it. I looked into Gilad's eyes and I looked at the almost frozen expression on his face. I knew I was looking at someone in terrible trauma, a trauma he would carry with him for the rest of his life. I was so happy to see his smile, to know he is free to do whatever he wanted with his friends in New York. But I also saw a man who had been held hostage for five years by the devil himself. The only thing I felt at that moment was pure happiness that Gilad Shalit was alive and here — with an opportunity to start his life again. I told myself it was worth it, it was worth everything.

I do not believe in negotiating with terrorists. And I do not believe Israel — or any country that fights terrorism — should ever do it again. But here was a human being right in front of me, and all he wanted to do was live. My heart went out to him completely.

"It's an honor and a pleasure to meet you, Gilad," I said. "I wish you all the best. Absolutely all the best." We continued to talk for a bit about New York and his plans in town. It was a very meaningful circle that was closed for me that night.

. . .

There are days when fighting against terrorism and advocating for its victims feels like trying to empty the ocean with an eyedropper. Just while I have been writing this book, hundreds more innocent adults and children have been murdered around the world. Some of those attacks received attention in the international news. Many did not. But each attack affected someone just like me or you — a person going about their daily lives, wanting nothing more than to care for their families in a moment of peace.

One of our great Jewish teachers who lived almost 2,000 years ago, Rabbi Tarfon, tells us that just because a task is enormous and we cannot complete it doesn't mean we should abdicate our responsibility to do what we can. I think about that message when the task I've taken on feels overwhelming. And I think about a girl named Martine.

Martine was one of the two French campers at One Heart Global whose friend was murdered while the three of them were on a school trip in Cairo. I could hardly imagine what it must have been like to be a 15-year-old in a foreign country without parents nearby, walking with a friend one moment only to have her killed by a bomb the next.

Martine was a very quiet girl, very shy, and initially spent most of her time at camp with the boy who had been with her in Cairo. When I spoke with her at length, I could see her kindness and sweetness. But understandably, she had grown a hard shell — the only way she knew to protect those soft places against even more pain. Her group psychologist had told us she had stopped paying attention in school. She had withdrawn from friends and family. Her mother, especially, was very concerned. During the week of summer camp, I saw Martine shed a bit of that hard shell. I saw her smiling, laughing, and spending more and more time with her new friends from other countries. When she left to go home, I felt hopeful for her.

In 2011, I went to France to speak at the International Congress for Victims of Terrorism. The date was September

14, my father's birthday. It was one of the most important days in my life — just an incredible honor to share my expertise about victims of terror and the support they need on behalf of my father on his birthday. I could hardly believe the perfect timing.

I was scheduled as one of the three speakers to open the conference and was also asked to answer questions from the European media. I felt such a great responsibility, wanting every word I said to be right.

As I started my answer to the very first question, I said, "It is a great honor for me to be here with you all today. It is such a special day to me, not only because I am a guest with so many survivors of terrorism, but also because today is my father's birthday. In his memory, and in memory of all our loved ones, I would like to start with a minute of silence to pray for all the victims who are no longer with us." The large room was completely silent. I looked at the people in front of me, some with their eyes closed, some with tears, others looking down or up. As we prayed, I spoke to my father and told him how much I missed him. It was one of the most honorable days in my life.

One day at the conference, a woman I did not recognize came right up to me with a big hug. I had met so many people that week and I tried to place this woman's face, but I just couldn't.

"Jacob!" She said my name as if we were long-lost friends. "Jacob, I'm Martine's mother. And you're the man who gave me my daughter back. The girl I sent to your camp was someone I hardly knew. But the girl who came home was Martine!" I looked at her, taking in her smile, her energy, her happiness. She gave me another big hug and kissed both of my cheeks. I explained that it was the other teens who had changed Martine's life, not me. But that was an unimportant distinction to this happy woman. Martine's mother and I spoke for about 30 minutes. The smile never left her face as she told me over and over how much Martine had changed and how happy their family was now. I was so happy, too! I knew this was just the beginning of bigger things to come for Martine.

Watching the happiness pour out of Martine's mother, I realized once again I was definitely on the right path for my life. I knew I wanted to help as many people as I possibly could during my lifetime. In fact, I just wished I could save the entire world.

That night, I went to dinner with Martine and her mother, our other camper from Paris, and his mother. We had a wonderful dinner, a wonderful time filled with love and laughter and a sense of intense connection that was almost difficult for me to believe.

All of us at the table that night had lost someone to a senseless, useless, indiscriminate act of violence. Yet, while the pain and terror of that loss were still there, here we were laughing — just as we should be. The pain will always be there, walking just beside us as we journey forward in our lives. But watching Martine and her friend that night, it was clear they realized their lives were bigger than the pain. Yes, they might trip over that pain occasionally in the bright futures I envision to be waiting for them. But they will no longer be defined by it. They will not be consumed by it.

I was overwhelmed by emotions that night as I looked around the table. What greater meaning could there be than to have contributed in even the smallest of ways to the healing of these teens? And I smiled. No one else at that table had the pleasure of knowing my father. Yet, all of us together were living the legacy of Rami Kimchy.

2015
Los Angeles

Dear Friends,

Our lives can change in one moment. That's all it takes for us to cross that line from happiness to pain, from innocence to a completely new way of seeing the world. But that moment can also be a great catalyst for growth, even if we hadn't planned on growing quite that quickly.

Sometimes I ask myself if I'm the same tough guy I used to be with my brown leather jacket, sports car, hair gel, and endless smile. To some who know me and to new people I meet daily, I am that person—happy, standing strong, and smiling. But to those who know my story, I am a different Jacob. They know I was forever changed by having seen the treacherous, cruel face of terrorism close up. Thirteen years later, I still confront those memories every day. To be a victim of terrorism is to live every day with pain, longing and loss. Those scars of pain and trauma are seared into my heart, and it is never over.

If that weren't enough, terrorism took away my precious father.

Every day, people suffer from physical accidents, sickness, financial disasters, family violence, emotional abuse, and significant challenges related to personal relationships, employment, chronic pain, disability, and general health.

No matter what causes the pain in your own life or in the life of someone you love, please know there is hope for your future! I want you to know you can learn how to find the light in your life, even if that is almost impossible to believe right now. There is a light for each of us to step into, no matter what.

Many of us need some help to get there. I certainly did.

Before I opened myself up to working with a social worker and to sharing my story in a support group, I thought being strong meant keeping my pain all locked up inside and presenting a "manly" face to the world no matter what, no matter how lost I felt. I thought I should be able to take care of all my pain on my own. Now, thankfully, I know better.

I want you to know what I learned: Being strong means knowing yourself, identifying your needs and advocating on your own behalf — caring for your own self so you can go out and help others in this world. You do have the power to do that.

You have a choice in front of you. Every morning can be a new sunrise in your life. But it's up to you to believe that everything you are going through can push you and motivate you to create a better life. You have the choice to decide where you want to be in your future. You can achieve strength and success as a result of your actions and the courage to look forward and say, "I can."

My mission in life is to help as many people as possible learn to say "I can," learn to find their own new sunrise. That is my father's legacy.

Please visit my website and contact me with any question or if you are in need of help. www.jacobkimchy.com.

Thank you,
Jacob Kimchy

ACKNOWLEDGMENTS

I would like to thank my wife, Alecia, who supported me throughout the process of A NEW SUNRISE and in everyday life. I am proud of her for the person she is today, moving on with the memories of 9/11.

My deep thanks goes to my siblings, Pazit and Moshe, who are both always a part of me even though we no longer live close by. They both showed me so much about the world we live in and are role models for me.

A special thanks goes to my nephew and niece (Yariv and Adi) for their love and smiles every time I see them, and for the fact that they cherish my father in their heart. Also, for going with me to the beach where I grew up and for taking this book's cover photo.

A huge thanks goes to Janis Dworkis for her help and support with the entire process of this book, for being warm, kind, professional, and for her patience.

I am grateful to have my Aunt Leah, who survived the Holocaust, now living in LA, inspiring the entire family, and uniting us all together.

I thank Barbara and Rafi for being a family to me when I lived in New York.

To all my uncles, aunties, cousins, friends, and supporters of One Heart,

I love you all.

ABOUT THE AUTHOR

Jacob Kimchy is a motivational speaker and life coach. Using his personal story and experiences to help others, he works one-on-one with individual trauma survivors and with large groups. He also advocates in the international arena for services for victims of terrorism and trauma, who rarely have access to the long-term physical- and mental-health support they need. Mr. Kimchy, who holds a bachelor's degree in business and a master's degree in management, lives in Southern California.

Visit www.JacobKimchy.com
Follow Jacob on Facebook
or Twitter at @JacobKimchy

20754311R00128

Made in the USA
San Bernardino, CA
22 April 2015